STORIES
ABOUT
PURGATORY

"It is therefore a holy and whole-
some thought to pray for the dead,
that they may be loosed from sins."
—2 Machabees 12:46

CMJ Marian Publishers
Distributors for *Direction for Our Times*
Tan Books and Other Publications

Toll Free 1-888-636-6799
Fax 708-636-2855

www.cmjbooks.com
P.O. Box 661, Oak Lawn, IL 60454

STORIES
ABOUT
PURGATORY
AND WHAT THEY REVEAL

---

30 DAYS
FOR THE HOLY SOULS

Compiled from Traditional Sources by
An Ursuline Nun of Sligo, Ireland

"Have pity on me, have pity on me,
at least you my friends, because the
hand of the Lord hath touched me."
—Job 19:21

TAN BOOKS AND PUBLISHERS, INC.
Rockford, Illinois 61105

Nihil Obstat: Richard A. O'Gorman, O.S.A.
                Censor Deputatus

Imprimatur: ✠ Francis
                Archbishop of Westminster
                September 14, 1904

First published in 1904, by R. & T. Washbourne, 1, 2 & 4 Paternoster Row, London, and Benziger Bros., New York, Cincinnati and Chicago, under the title *Forget-Me-Nots from Many Gardens, or Thirty Days' Devotion to the Holy Souls*. Retypeset, retitled and republished in 2005 by TAN Books and Publishers, Inc.

ISBN 0-89555-799-1

Cover illustration: Detail of stained-glass window *Assumption of Our Lady*. Photo copyright © 1992 Alan Brown. Used by arrangement with Al Brown Photo, 3597 N. Roberts Rd., Bardstown, Kentucky 40004.

Printed and bound in the United States of America.

TAN BOOKS AND PUBLISHERS, INC.
P.O. Box 424
Rockford, Illinois 61105
2005

Rest Eternal Grant Them, Lord!

Take we up the touching burden of
  November plaints,
Pleading for the Holy Souls,
  God's yet uncrowned Saints.
Still unpaid to our departed
  is the debt we owe;
Still unransomed, some are pining,
  sore oppressed with woe.
Friends we loved and vowed to cherish
  call us in their need:
Prove we now our love was real,
  true in word and deed.
"Rest eternal grant them, Lord!"
  full often let us pray—
"Requiem æternam dona eis, Domine!"

Requiem Aeternam

Requiem aeternam dona eis Domine: et lux perpetua luceat eis. Requiescant in pace. Amen.

Eternal Rest

Eternal rest grant unto them, O Lord, and let perpetual light shine upon them. May they rest in peace. Amen.

Contents

STORIES
ABOUT
PURGATORY

"Amen I say to you, as long as you did it to one of these my least brethren, you did it to me."
—Matthew 25:40

❧ FIRST DAY ❧

A Day of Fervent Prayer that
Many Souls in Purgatory
May Be Admitted to the Joys of Paradise

ALL Saints—All Souls! It was well done to place thus close together these two beautiful solemnities. There is a fitness, too, in this season of the fall of the leaf for such a commemoration of the departed. The flowers and green leaves of May, the yellow harvests and the warm glow of August, would be out of place upon All Souls' Day. Better to sing this universal Requiem when Nature herself has laid aside the garments of her gladness, when the warm blood of youth is no longer coursing through the earth's veins, when the very sunshine seems chill and sad, and the wind through the naked branches is a dirge. But at whatever period they come, All Saints Day [November 1] and All Souls Day [November 2] should come together. And they come together, though one might be tempted, in all reverence, to wish that the order of their coming were reversed. If the commemoration of All Souls came first, we might hope that the suffrages of all the Church Militant on that day, joined with the prayers of all the Church Triumphant, might avail much to the relief of the Suffering Church; might procure the discharge of many, perhaps, among the patient victims detained in that prison house of mercy, and so increase the hosts of those honored in the Festival of All Saints. Or is it only by a tender afterthought, as it were, that the Church, having rejoiced in the glory of those of her children who have secured their

1

crown in Heaven, turns with affectionate compassion to those others who are not yet *there,* though they are no longer *here,* whose earthly fight is over, but whose heavenly happiness is not yet attained? Would that all who are gone were gone to join that multitude which no man can number, thronging the Courts of Heaven! But so many disappoint the yearnings of the Heart of Jesus. So many live and die as if Jesus had not lived and died for them. And even of those who die in the grace of Our Lord Jesus Christ, how few are found "with the perfect sheen of Heaven upon them"! How few are pure enough, at once, after closing their eyes upon this sinful world, to open them to the full piercing light of glory, to meet, without shrinking, the all-discerning Eye of the God of Infinite Purity! And we are living under that same Eye, and we are laboring for that Heaven which the Saints have not earned too dearly, and for which the Holy Souls are not undergoing too severe a preparation. Have we worked and prayed during the past year as if we believed this?

These and other general lessons are urged upon us by the twin feasts with which November opens—if, indeed, the 2nd of November can be called a feast—a more eager longing for the society of the blessed in Heaven, a deeper horror for sin, a keener thirst for the glory of God and for the increase of grace and merit in our own souls, and a more intense reverence for the majesty and holiness of God thus "wonderful in His Saints," and thus rigid in the purification of the Holy Souls.

But there is for each of these solemnities one peculiar object having its counterpart amongst the objects of the other. As All Saints' Day may well be supposed to offer compensation to such of the blessed as have no special festival during the year, so the suffrages of All Souls' Day supply what is wanting in the individual charity of the faithful, and may be devoted chiefly to the most neglected of the Holy Souls—those who have no friends to pray for them. No doubt there are many such: some with no loving hearts to cherish their memory—and even the most loving hearts cannot keep up a practical remembrance of the departed during many years of our short lifetime. The Purgatory of many souls may last very many lifetimes. One who is hardly there now, for he ended a very holy life by a very holy death, said on his deathbed: "Eternity is so long that I think Purgatory must be long, too. You must help me, then, with prayers. Even in religion we are apt to forget our deceased brothers, relying too much on their having died religious."

Before the month closes which is opening now, may our hearts have grown more pleasing to the Heart of Jesus and the Heart of Mary—more dear to them because more like to them; and, as all belongs to Jesus, let us give to Mary a mother's share in all the days of our lives, especially in these two sacred days which invite us to love and honor her as Queen of All Saints and Compassionate Mother of the Suffering Souls.

> "Ah! turn to Jesus, Mother! turn,
> And call Him by His tenderest names.
> Pray for the holy souls that burn
> This hour amid the cleansing flames."
> —Rev. Matthew Russell, S.J.

On one occasion as the community over which St. Gertrude presided recited the Great Psalter for the souls of the faithful departed, the Saint prepared herself for Holy Communion, and prayed for these souls with great fervor. She then asked Our Lord why this Psalter was so acceptable to Him, and why it obtained such great relief for the souls, since the immense number of psalms which were recited and the long prayers after each caused more weariness than devotion. Our Lord replied: "The desire which I have for the deliverance of the souls makes it acceptable to Me; even as a prince who had been obliged to imprison one of his nobles to whom he was much attached, and was compelled by his justice to refuse him pardon, would most thankfully avail himself of the intercession and satisfaction of others to release his friend, thus do I act toward those whom I have redeemed by My death and Precious Blood, rejoicing in the opportunity of releasing them from their pains and bringing them to eternal joys." "But," continued the Saint, "is the labor of those who recite this Psalter acceptable to Thee?" He replied: "My love renders it most agreeable to Me; and if a soul is released thereby, I accept it as if I had been Myself delivered from captivity, and I will assuredly reward this act at a fitting time according to the abundance of My mercy." Then she inquired: "How many souls are released by these prayers?" He answered: "The number is proportioned to the zeal and fervour of those who pray for them." He added: "My love urges Me to release a great number of souls for the prayers of each religious."

A short offering which may be made each morning for the souls in Purgatory:

O my God, deign to accept my every thought, word, and action as a loving petition to Thy mercy on behalf of the suffering souls in Purgatory, particularly _____. I unite to Thy Sacred Passion the trials and contradictions of this day, which I purpose to bear with patience, in expiation for the sins and infidelities which retain Thy children in the purifying flames of Purgatory. Amen.

⌒ SECOND DAY ⌒

A Day of Supplication for
All the Faithful Departed

THE month of November, with its devotion to the Holy Souls, comes again to remind us of an essential obligation of charity, binding upon all who care to claim their part in the Communion of Saints—in the great family of Jesus Christ—the elect of God, gathered from East and West. Hearts that truly beat in unison with the Sacred Heart of Jesus and the Immaculate Heart of Mary cannot turn away with indifference from that touching cry for help: "Have pity on me! have pity on me! at least you, my friends!" If hitherto we have thought too little of those "who have gone before us with the sign of faith," if we have been like the rest of men wrapped up in the thought of self, immersed in the trifles of today, forgetful of those whose lives were once closely linked with ours, and *should* be still, now in the month of the Holy Souls we may "rise to better things," to truer thoughts of life, to a deeper sense of the value of time, to a fuller understanding of the will of God in our regard, and especially to an appreciation, altogether new, of the solicitous service which the Church Militant on earth owes to the Church Suffering in Purgatory.

Not because in serving others we shall most securely serve ourselves, nor yet because we hope to secure the gratitude of Saints who soon will reign with God in Heaven; but because those who are now in the cleansing fires are of our own flesh and blood, our brothers and sisters in Jesus Christ, we will do what we can to help them from this time forward, regretting if we have been negligent till now. It should be enough for us to know that those who have a claim upon our love are stretching out their hands to us for help, and crying: *"Have pity on me!"* Yet to remember the dead with anything beyond a transient thought is the exception, and to leave them in God's hands to pay their debt, after making a few feeble efforts to help them in the first days of our bereavement, is the rule. Such conduct is almost as usual as it is unreasonable. Those who thus forget parents and brethren and friends may fear that they will be in their turn forgotten, for God keeps His mercy for the merciful.

While dear friends are with us we flatter ourselves that we love them with a disinterested love; that in doing them good service we are not thinking of ourselves at all; that we are even willing to submit to much inconvenience for their sake. And all the while it is too often our own satisfaction that we seek, even in our self-sacrifice, rendering kind offices, not for sake of the good we do thereby, but for the happiness which accrues to ourselves, as men give alms sometimes from no higher motive than is found in the pleasure of giving. It is not true that all human friendship is thus infected with selfishness, but a great deal of that which looks like the pure gold of charity is not such. The value of our friendship in the present may be estimated by its value in the past. Our treatment of the dead will serve us for the touchstone of the sincerity and purity of our affection. "The heart that has truly loved never forgets."

Those who once were dearly loved—our playmates in childhood, our chosen companions in later life, who sat at the same table, who knelt at the same shrine, who shared our joys and sorrows, and, it may be, now and again spoke to us of death and eternity, with wondering words about that other world, and who then passed from our sight into that other world—are they remembered now? Do we pray for them or to them? Or are they in good truth, if we must be honest with ourselves, really nothing more to us now than faces that look upon us in a dream? Is their connection with us a reality of our present life, or are they merely creatures of the past, belonging to a state of things which has vanished from our hearts and minds? According to our answer must be the estimate which we form of the generosity with which we love our friends and help our fellow creatures.

The Holy Souls in Purgatory are unutterably dear to God,

because of all the graces and merits they have won and can never lose, and because of the keen sufferings which they are bearing with such heavenly patience in their love of Him, and their desire to be more worthy of Him. The Virgin Mother watches with a mother's holy anxiety while the last faint traces and shades of sin fade off from each beautiful soul, longing for the moment when all shall be paid, and these her dear children received into their long-expected happiness. St. Joseph, the particular patron of these patient holy ones, is eagerly looking forward to the moment when he may bear his charges into the Father's bosom. And think you that God and Our Lady and St. Joseph will not love and bless those who by their holy liberality shall hasten that moment which they all so earnestly desire? And when those benefactors shall send their petitions through Purgatory and some dear sufferer shall cry to Heaven, "Grant them what they ask for, for they have done great things for us," can you think the prayer will be unheard?

See what St. Catherine of Bologna used to say on this subject. "When I wish," she said, "to obtain some favor from the Eternal Father, I invoke the souls in their place of expiation, and charge them with the petition I have to make to Him, and I feel I am heard through their means." This ought to be a great encouragement to us, and doubtless it will be. It is such an easy way of pleasing God and winning blessings for ourselves to make little compacts with the suffering souls that we will daily perform some indulgenced exercise for their relief, and that they in return will forward our particular intentions.

Prayer for the Holy Souls is a most fruitful devotion for all, but especially for those who have lost some dear relation, some friend, or someone in whom they took an intense interest, and who they conjecture may still be detained in the purifying fire. Let me give a few words from the third of Lady Georgiana Fullerton's letters about the "Helpers of the Holy Souls," which relate to this subject:

"Amongst the Helpers of the Holy Souls," she writes, "several have made great sacrifices to God in order to obtain mercy for souls long ago called away from this world. We can all imitate their example. 'Oh, if it were not too late!' is the cry of many a heart tortured by anxiety regarding the fate of some loved one who died apparently out of the Church, or not in the state of grace. We answer: It is never too late. Pray, work, suffer. The Lord foresaw your efforts. The Lord knew what was to come, and may have given to that soul at its last hour some extraordinary graces which snatched it from destruction and placed it in safety, where your love may still reach it, your prayers relieve, your sacrifices avail."

Many religious orders have in all ages distinguished themselves by their works of charity toward the poor, and have on this account received universal approbation; but the monks of Cluny have distinguished themselves by their suffrages for the souls of the faithful departed, for which they have received the commendation of the whole Catholic world. The circumstance is related by Cardinal Baronius as follows: A revelation having been made to several servants of God that many souls were freed from Purgatory through the prayers of the monks of Cluny, who among all the faithful distinguished themselves in this holy exercise, their abbot, St. Odilo, about the year of Our Lord 1040, determined to promote this work of pre-eminent charity to a much greater extent. He therefore ordered that, besides the ordinary suffrages and prayers which his monks daily offered for the purpose, the Holy Sacrifice should be offered on a certain fixed day in all the monasteries of his Order in behalf of these souls, which custom was afterwards taken up by the whole Church—the Commemoration of the Second of November being thereby instituted.

St. Malachy, Archbishop of Armagh, conversing one day with his disciples, the subject turned on death, and each person was asked where and when he would like to end his days, supposing it were his fate to die away from his own country. Various were the answers. One person designated such a place and such a time, another a different time and place, each according to his peculiar views and line of reasoning. When it came to the Saint's turn, he said that he would select the Monastery of Clairvaux, a place conspicuous for its love of rule and spirit of fervent charity; and as to the time, he would prefer the day of solemn Commemoration of all the Faithful Departed—to the end, he said, that he might share in the advantage of all the prayers offered on such an occasion in that abode of sanctity. Nor was he disappointed in his desire, for being on his way to visit the Sovereign Pontiff, Eugenius III, a short time after, he became seriously ill on arriving at Clairvaux and perceived that his end was approaching. Then, raising his eyes to Heaven in gratitude, he cried out with the Psalmist: "This is my rest for ever: here will I dwell, for I have chosen it."

On the morning of the 2nd of November the intensity of the fever increased to such a degree that death ensued, and his soul, released from its earthly prison, and accompanied by the fervent prayers of the monks and the faithful, and surrounded by a multitude of Holy Souls whom these suffrages had released from Purgatory, presented itself before the tribunal of Jesus Christ to receive the crown of eternal glory.

At the obsequies of St. Malachy, St. Bernard, offering a Requiem Mass for the repose of the soul of his holy friend, added to the Mass a Collect to implore the Divine assistance through his intercession, having been assured of his glory by Divine revelation during the celebration of the Holy Sacrifice.

❧ THIRD DAY ❧

A Day of Prayer for Those Who Suffer Most in Purgatory

IT is certain that a person's sufferings in Purgatory are proportioned to his guilt; and as many are liable to depart this life great debtors to the Divine Justice on account of numerous venial sins and carelessness in atoning for mortal sins, let us this day remember those who *suffer most* in that place of torments.

Were we to say that the suffering endured in Purgatory included all the torments arising from all bodily diseases, we should give a terrifying idea of their violence; but St. Augustine, St. Gregory, and other Fathers say that our conception would fall very short of the reality, since the torments endured there are incomparably greater than those of the most violent diseases, united with all that could be inflicted by every possible instrument of torture. When we read in Church history of what the holy martyrs have endured for the Faith, when we reflect on the torments which the cruelty of barbarians has invented to torture their fellow men, we shudder with horror, we tremble with alarm, and yet the pains of Purgatory, as was revealed to St. Mary Magdalen de Pazzi, are incomparably greater.

Do not say that you have no apprehension of Purgatory because those who are confined there are sure of being saved, for though this certainly is a source of indescribable consolation, it does not hinder the sufferings which they continually endure. You will easily conceive this if you consider that though the holy Soul of Our Blessed Lord enjoyed that glory which belonged to it from all eternity, yet this enjoyment in the superior part did not prevent the inferior part from feeling in all their rigor the dreadful torments of His bitter Passion. "All that we can form an idea of," says St. Augustine, "is nothing in comparison to the pains of Purgatory; neither the eye has seen, nor the ear heard, anything like to them." St. Thomas says: "The flames of Purgatory are of the same nature as those of Hell, and hence they act, not by a natural movement, but as instruments of the Divine Justice, which is, as it were, the fire of these fires, and endows them with a force which they intrinsically do not possess."

It is to Purgatory we can best apply the words of Isaias: "The breath of the Lord as a torrent destroys the nations," for as the breath of the Lord is the Holy Ghost, the substantial love of the Father and the Son, and as great love occasions great hatred to what is opposed to it, and great hatred great chastisements, this Holy Spirit Himself avenges sin; and as He is God, punishes it as God. Hence it is that all the torments inflicted by men could not equal those of Purgatory, for what would the efforts of creatures be to the omnipotence of God, which is here employed in punishing?

The Poor Souls so suffering are incapable of helping themselves. On earth, even in the midst of our greatest trials, we can form no idea of such a state. The unfortunate being abandoned by all can sometimes still find in himself some resource, and if his right hand fail him can use the left; and should both be useless, he can always take refuge in his heart, where God waits for him. Each one of his sighs can become an act of love, each one of his pains a sacrifice, and his tears a treasure for eternity. But to suffer, and always to suffer, to weep tears of fire, and to feel that beneath the burning dew of these tears nothing but sufferings upon sufferings will come forth, until the hour marked by Divine Justice shall arrive; to be obliged to say, like a captive who can neither advance the hour of his deliverance nor open his prison door, "I can do nothing, nothing, to shorten the time of my trial"—such a state as this should certainly excite our compassion.

We have it in our power to help these suffering friends of God. We can do so by prayer, almsdeeds, the Holy Mass, and Indulgences, and to do so is certainly a work of mercy and charity. Understanding this full well, the Saints, without exception, have been most earnest and constant in their efforts to help them. Some of them have made this devotion one of the strong characteristics of their sanctity, and we venture to say that no truly devout or sincere Catholic neglects this spiritual work of mercy.

In Ireland this devotion has obtained a strong hold on the faithful, and whatever else the Irish may be wanting in, they cannot be accused of indifference toward their deceased friends. Even the very poor make many sacrifices in order to secure for their departed relatives, and others also, the special benefits of the Holy Mass. May the same enlightened piety ever remain firmly rooted in the hearts of our people, and may the day never come when they will cease to follow beyond the grave with tender solicitude the souls of those they loved in life.

In praying for the dead and gaining Indulgences for them, let us remember that every prayer we say, every sacrifice we make, every alms we give for the repose of the dear departed ones will all return upon ourselves in hundredfold blessings. They are God's friends, dear to His Sacred Heart, living in His grace and in constant communion with Him; and though they may not alleviate their own sufferings, their prayers in our behalf always avail. They can aid us most efficaciously. God will not turn a deaf ear to their intercession. Being Holy Souls, they are grateful souls. The friends that aid them, they in turn will also aid. We need not fear praying to them in all faith and confidence. They will obtain for us the special favors we desire. They will watch over us lovingly and tenderly; they will guard our steps; they will warn us against evil; they will shield us in moments of trial and danger; and when our hour of purgatorial suffering comes, they will use their influence in our behalf to assuage our pains and shorten the period of our separation from the Godhead.

———————

St. Malachy, having lost his sister by death, offered many fervent prayers and pious suffrages for her eternal repose. Having after some time desisted from doing so, he heard one night an unknown voice say to him that his sister waited outside the church and asked him for assistance. The Saint well understood what the needs of his sister were, and having resumed the pious exercises which he had discontinued, he saw her some time after at the entrance of the church in robes of mourning, and having a sad and disconsolate aspect. This vision caused him to redouble his prayers in her behalf, nor did he allow any day to pass without performing many acts of piety for her relief.

The soul on its next appearance had a less mournful garb and was inside the church, but durst not approach the altar. The Saint, having his confidence in the efficacy of his suffrages thus sustained, multiplied them even more than before, and did his utmost to satisfy the Divine Justice in her behalf. On her third appearance, he was consoled with the assurance that his pious intention had been effected. He saw her clad in garments of dazzling brightness, and advancing to the altar surrounded by a joyous band of blessed spirits, thus signifying to her holy brother that she had obtained admission into Heaven.

The various states or stages in which this soul appeared teach us the ordinary economy of God's providence—that He does not ordinarily liberate souls from Purgatory by an absolute act of His power and will, but exacts from them with the strictest justice the full payment of their debt, ever accepting the suffrages of the faithful in their behalf—which succors are the more advantageous to these poor souls the more frequently and fervently they are offered.

◈ FOURTH DAY ◈

A Day of Prayer for the Souls
Longest in Purgatory

T HE rigor of the purifying flames is so great that one moment of their endurance is more pain-inflicting than many years of severe penance in this world. What, then, must not those Poor Souls have undergone who have spent the longest time in that place of torture? Let us try today to alleviate their sufferings and abridge their exile.

We all expect, doubtless, or think ourselves sure, to go to Purgatory. If we do not think much of the matter at all, then we may have some vague notion of going straight to Heaven as soon as we are judged. But if we seriously reflect upon it—upon our own lives, upon God's sanctity, upon what we read in books of devotion and the lives of the Saints—I can hardly conceive any one of us expecting to escape Purgatory, and not, rather, feeling that it must be almost a stretch of the Divine mercy which will get us even there.

Now, if we really expect that our road to Heaven will be through the punishments of Purgatory—for surely its purification is penal—it very much concerns us to know the views of this state that appear to prevail in the Church. These views agree that the pains are extremely severe, as well because of the office which God intends them to fulfill, as because of the disembodied soul being the subject of them. They agree, also, with regard to the length of the suffering. This requires to be dwelt upon, as it is hard to convince people of it, and a great deal comes of the conviction, both to ourselves and others.

This duration may be understood in two ways: 1) as of actual length of time; and 2) as of seeming length from the excess of pain. With regard to the first, if we look into the revelations of Sister Francesca of Pampeluna, we shall find among some hundreds of cases that by far the greater majority suffered thirty, forty, or sixty years. Here are some of the examples: A holy bishop, for some negligence in his high office, had been in Purgatory fifty-nine years before he appeared to the servant of God; another bishop, so generous of his revenues that he was named "the almsgiver," had been there five years because he had wished for the dignity; a priest forty years because through his negligence some sick persons had died without the Sacraments; another forty-five years for inconsiderateness in his ministerial functions; a gentleman fifty-nine years for worldliness; another sixty-four for a fondness for playing at cards for money; another thirty-five years for worldliness.

Without multiplying instances, which it would be easy to do, these disclosures may teach us greater watchfulness over ourselves, and more unwearied perseverance in praying for the departed. The old foundations for perpetual Masses embody the same sentiment. We are apt to leave off too soon, imagining with a foolish and unenlightened fondness that our friends are freed from Purgatory much sooner than they really are. If Sister Francesca beheld the souls of many fervent Carmelites, some of whom had wrought miracles during life, still in Purgatory ten, twenty, thirty, sixty years after their death, and yet not near their deliverance, as many told her, what must become of us and ours? Then, as to seeming length from the extremity of pain, there are many instances on record in the Chronicles of the Franciscans, the Life of St. Francis Jerome, and elsewhere, of souls appearing an hour or two after death, and thinking they had been many years in Purgatory. Such may be the Purgatory of those who are caught up to meet the Lord at the Last Day.

We are also told that what we in the world call very trivial faults are most severely visited in Purgatory. St. Peter Damian gives us many instances of this, and others are collected and quoted by Bellarmine. Slight feelings of self-complacency, trifling inattentions in the recital of the Divine Office, and the like, occur frequently among them.

Sister Francesca mentions the case of a girl of fourteen in Purgatory because she was not quite conformed to the will of God in dying so young. And one soul said to her: "Ah, men little think in the world how dearly they are going to pay here for faults they hardly note there!" She even saw souls that were immensely punished only for having been scrupulous in this life—either, I suppose, because there is mostly self-will in scruples, or because they did not lay them down when obedience commanded. Wrong notions about small faults may thus lead us to neglect the dead, or leave off our prayers too soon, as well as lose a lesson for ourselves.

Consider the helplessness of the Holy Souls. They lie like the paralytic at the pool. It would seem as if even the coming of the Angel were not an effectual blessing to them, unless there be some one of us to help them. Some have even thought they cannot pray. Anyhow, they have no means of making themselves heard by us on whose charity they depend. Some writers have said that Our Blessed Lord will not help them without our co-operation; and that Our Blessed Lady cannot help them except in indirect ways, because she is no longer able to make satisfaction, though I never like to hear of anything our dearest Mother cannot do, and I regard such statements with suspicion.

Another feature in their helplessness is the forgetfulness of the living or the cruel flattery of relations, who will always have it that those near or dear to them die the death of saints. They would surely have a scruple if they knew of how many Masses and prayers they rob the souls by the selfish exaggeration of their goodness. I call it selfish, for it is nothing more than a miserable device to console themselves in their sorrow. The very state of the Holy Souls is one of the most unbounded helplessness. They cannot do penance; they cannot merit; they cannot satisfy; they cannot gain indulgences; they have no Sacraments; they are not under the jurisdiction of God's Vicar, overflowing with the plenitude of means of grace and manifold benedictions. They are a portion of the Church without either priesthood or altar at their own command.

How numerous are the lessons we may learn from these considerations, on our own behalf as well as on behalf of the Holy Souls! For ourselves, what light does all this throw on slovenliness, lukewarmness, and love of ease? What does it make us think of performing our devotions out of a mere spirit of formality or a trick of habit? What a change should it not work in our lives! What diligence in our examens, Confessions, Communions and prayers! It seems as if the grace of all graces for which we should be ever importuning our dear Lord would be to hate sin with something of the hatred wherewith He hated it in the Garden of Gethsemane.

Oh, is not the purity of God something awful, unspeakable, adorable? He who is Himself a simple act has gone on acting, multiplying acts, since creation, yet He has incurred no stain! He is ever mingling with a most unutterable condescension with what is beneath Him—yet no stain! He loves His creatures with a love immeasurably more intense than the wildest passions of earth—yet no stain! He is omnipotent, yet it is beyond the limits of His power to receive a stain. He is so pure that the very vision of Him causes eternal purity and blessedness. Mary's purity is but a fair, thin shadow of it. Nay, the Sacred Humanity itself cannot adequately worship the purity of the Most High, and we, even we, are to dwell in His arms forever; we are to dwell amid the everlasting burnings of that Uncreated Purity! Yet, let us look at our lives; let us trace our hearts faithfully through but one day, and see of what mixed intentions, human respect, self-love and pusillanimous temper our actions—nay, even our devotions—are made up; and does not Purgatory, heated sevenfold and endured to the day of doom, seem but a gentle novitiate for the Vision of the All-Holy?

But we not only learn lessons for our own good, but for the good of the Holy Souls. We see that our charitable attentions toward them must be far more vigorous and persevering than they have been; for that people go to Purgatory for very little matters, and remain there an unexpectedly long time. Their most touching appeal to us lies in their help-lessness; and our dear Lord, with His usual loving arrange-ment, has made the extent of our power to help them more than commensurate with their inability to help themselves. We can make over to them, by way of suffrage, the indul-gences we gain, provided the Church has made them applic-able to the dead. We can limit and direct upon them the intention of the Adorable Sacrifice. We can give to them all the satisfactions of our ordinary actions and of our suffer-ings, and in many other ways we can help the suffering souls.   —FATHER FABER

———————————

It is related of a religious of St. Dominic that, finding himself at the point of death, he earnestly begged a friend who was a priest to have the goodness, as soon as he was dead, to offer the Holy Sacrifice of the Mass for the repose of his soul. He had scarcely expired when the priest went to the church and celebrated Mass with devotion for this intention. The Holy Sacrifice being over, he had scarcely taken off the sacred vestments when the deceased religious presented himself to him and rebuked him severely for his hardness of heart in leaving him in the most cruel fire of Purgatory for the long space of thirty years. "How thirty years?" asked the good priest, in amazement. "Why, it is not yet an hour since you departed this life, so that your corpse is, so to say, still warm." To this the poor soul replied: "Learn hence, my friend, how tormenting is the fire of Purgatory when scarcely an hour seems to be thirty years, and learn, too, to have pity on us."

∽ FIFTH DAY ∾

A Day of Prayer for Deceased Parents And Relatives

IT should seem unnecessary to urge you to pray fervently for those to whom you owe so much. Nature, reason, religion, all loudly claim your suffrages in their behalf.

————————

Hope is alternately the support and torture of the human heart. None have such assured ground for hope as the souls in Purgatory, and none at the same time experience so intensely the opposite effects of this potent sentiment. The object of their hope is God Himself, who promises and gives Himself as the recompense of the just; and if the assurance of having their present sufferings so gloriously rewarded imparted to the Saints an unutterable joy in the midst of trials and adversities, how much more consoled and fortified must not the Holy Souls feel, even in their prison of dolors, from the thought that God will shortly assuage their sufferings and reward them with unspeakable delights! Why do we not in the trials of life also raise our eyes to Heaven, and accustom ourselves to bear patiently our crosses, which, if so borne, shall be rewarded with eternal glory in Paradise?

Hope consoles us in proportion as it is the more assured. Who, then, can express the consolation the Holy Souls derive from their certainty of possessing God hereafter? They read in the decrees of God that they are the elect of His eternal kingdom. Calling to mind the promises of Jesus Christ, and being in possession of His grace, they cannot for a moment doubt that they are to be the coheirs of His happiness and glory. They consider their deeds of justice, and expect with unwavering confidence the crown of immortality with which the Lord, the Just Judge, shall reward their merits. Their hope is so solidly based on this triple foundation that it not only does not admit of doubt or fear, but has all the force of immediate and absolute possession.

But although the suffering souls are thus assured of possessing God, He still defers communicating Himself to them until they shall have been completely freed from every stain of sin. He wills also that this very delay should increase the ardor of their desires. Thus, on the one hand the certainty of their hope sustains and fortifies them, while the delay of possession, on the other hand, afflicts them, and those very desires which are the food and life of their hope serve to afflict and torture them most keenly. The more exalted the object of their hope, the more painful in proportion is their punishment, and its violence increases with the intensity of their love. "I speak not," says St. Austin, "to those that are cold and insensible, but give me a heart that aspires to the Sovereign Good, and it will feel the meaning of my words."

One great advantage arising from the thought of Purgatory is that it inspires with a spirit of penance and self-denial; for it reminds us that Divine Justice, though severe, is not blind, and never punishes the same fault twice, since if expiation is made in this world, it will not be required in the next. Knowing that justice so inflexible and unrelenting in Purgatory is easily disarmed here on earth, we naturally feel an earnest desire to escape the terrible fire of Purgatory, which can only punish sins unexpiated, and consequently we take care to leave few stains to be cleansed away hereafter.

God in His infinite goodness affords us the opportunity of paying the debt contracted by a deliberate act by means of a voluntary satisfaction, and only chastises us in the other world because we have not had the courage to punish ourselves in this. Our interest, therefore, lies in forestalling His judgments and justice by self-imposed penances, for however severe they may be, they fall far short of those of Purgatory. This thought fills the soul with a holy courage to embrace mortification and penance generously, saying: "Better settle now my accounts with God; better take advantage of His mercy to satisfy His justice; better pay my debts now while I can do so easily. This is my resolve and firm determination."

Another advantage arising from the thought of Purgatory is that it renders us more patient and courageous in bearing the trials and sufferings of this life, and teaches us to look upon them as means given us by God in His Divine mercy to make up for what is wanting in our penances, and thus escape the terrible expiation of Purgatory. Happy are they that understand this truth; not only will they receive the crosses Divine Providence sends them with resignation, but even with joy and gratitude, regarding them as signal marks of the goodness of Our Lord, as golden coins with which to pay a portion of their debts. No matter what may be the nature and duration of their sufferings, they learn to endure them peacefully, always remembering that thereby they acquire great merit. "But," says Fénelon, "human nature seeks to escape Purgatory both here and hereafter, with this result: that it renders useless our satisfaction here below, and we have after death still to endure the pains of Purgatory. Were we now, like the Holy Souls, to remain peaceful and patient in the hands of God, we should be purified by the fire of His love."

Let us not forget that the trials and sufferings of this life are a real Purgatory, and that the soul weighed down by the cross is as truly purified as are the souls in Purgatory by its cleansing flames. But if we repine and murmur against God by impatience, we only render ourselves more guilty in His sight, and abuse the precious gift of suffering He bestows upon us to expiate sin. Let us, then, suffer as the Saints suffered, as the souls in Purgatory suffer, and our sufferings will have the double advantage of purifying us and enabling us to gain merit.

The habitual remembrance of Purgatory keeps up the fervor of the just, rendering them more watchful over themselves, more attentive in the fulfillment of all their duties toward God, their neighbor, and themselves, more careful in the performance of the most trifling actions, in purifying

their intention, and always acting for the greater glory of
God.

Finally, the thought of Purgatory inspires us with charity
for the Holy Souls detained there. The remembrance of their
sufferings fills us with tender compassion for them, which
quickly manifests itself in giving them aid and relief, in praying for them, in offering acts of self-denial in their favor, and
making use of all the means at our disposal to relieve them.
Their interests become ours in a certain manner; their sufferings, if I may so speak, become ours; the agony of their separation from God creates within us a holy impatience to open
for them the gates of their heavenly country. Thus do we,
even unconsciously to ourselves, practice the virtue of charity
in the most perfect and heroic degree, and, whilst thinking
we are only working for others, enrich ourselves with abundant merits; while paying the debts of the souls to whom we
are devoted, we at the same time discharge our own, since
charity is the most excellent of all virtues, making up before
God for all the rest. Therefore, those who practice it toward
the dead, far from losing, gain by it, God in a wonderful manner rewarding those who help His friends.

THE WAITING SOULS

> They are waiting for our petitions,
>   Silent and calm;
> Their lips no prayer can utter,
>   No suppliant psalm.
> We have made them all too weary,
>   With long delay;
> For the souls in their still agony
>   Pray—fervently pray:
>   *Requiescant in pace.*
>
> For the souls thou holdest dearest,
>   Let prayers arise;
> The voice of love is mighty,
>   And will pierce the skies.

Waste not in selfish weeping
  One precious day,
But speeding thy love to Heaven,
  Pray—fervently pray:
        Requiescant in pace.

For the soul by all forgotten,
  Even its own—
By its nearest and its dearest,
  Left all alone—
Whisper a *De Profundis*,
  Or gently lay
Alms in some poor one's outstretched palm,
  Pray—fervently pray:
        Requiescant in pace.

For the soul that is nearest Heaven,
  That sees the gate
Even now ajar, and the light within,
  And yet must wait,
Ere the Angels come to convoy it,
  In bright array;
For the eager soul so near to joy,
  Pray—fervently pray:
        Requiescant in pace.

For the soul that most loved Our Lady,
  For Our Lady's love,
Speed with thy supplications
  To its home above;
And our Mother in benediction
  Her hand will lay
Tenderly on thy bowed down head.
  Pray—fervently pray:
        Requiescant in pace.

For the love of the Heart of Jesus—
  They love it too—

By all sweet home affections
   That once they knew,
As thou hopest in thy utmost need
   To find thy stay
In the prayers of those who loved thee once,
   Pray—fervently pray:
      Requiescant in pace.

There are few souls, even of the just, who directly after this life pass immediately to the eternal joys of Heaven. Even the imperfections of the Saints have to be cleansed by fire. The following example, related by St. Peter Damian, will serve to prove this: St. Severinus, Archbishop of Cologne, was a prelate of such extraordinary sanctity that God vouchsafed to distinguish him by remarkable miracles. After his death the Saint appeared one day to a canon of Cologne Cathedral in a small branch of the Rhine, in which he stood plunged up to the waist. The Canon asked him why he stood there in the water—as on account of his extraordinary sanctity he ought to be reigning gloriously in Heaven. "If you wish to know," replied the Saint, "give me your hand, in order that you may understand the pain which I suffer, not by hearing of it, but by touch." Then, having seized his hand, he dipped it gently into the water. Though he drew it rapidly out, so great was the heat that he felt from it that the flesh fell off scorched, and the bare bones held together by the joints were in great pain. Then the Saint said: "I do not suffer this great torment for anything more than for having recited the Canonical Hours hastily and with distraction. For while I was counsellor in the Emperor's court, having a great deal of business, I did not recite the Divine Office at the proper hours or with devotion. This is my own fault." Then, begging the Canon to join with him in prayer to obtain the cure of his hand, and beseeching him to obtain his own liberation from such great sufferings by the suffrage of prayers, alms and Masses, he suddenly disappeared, leaving the priest miraculously cured and full of fear of God's judgments.

∽ SIXTH DAY ∾

A Day of Prayer for Deceased
Friends and Benefactors

L ET us spend this day in supplication for those who while on earth befriended us, and were even ready to make sacrifices for our happiness.

It is a very common belief that the souls in Purgatory, though they have no power to aid themselves, can obtain many graces for the living. The celebrated theologian Suarez says: "The souls in Purgatory are holy and dear to God. Their charity compels them to love us, and they know—at least, in a general manner—to what perils we are exposed, and what particular graces we most need from the Divine bounty. Why should they not intercede for us, even though they have still to expiate on their own behalf? In this life are we not all debtors to God? Yet, nevertheless, this does not hinder us from praying for our neighbor. Did not the holy patriarchs and prophets reposing in Abraham's bosom from the depths of Limbo pray for the living on earth?"

Leaving aside the graver testimonies of the Fathers of the Church, will not Catholic piety in doubtful cases solve at once the question? How many times have we not heard it said, and that even by persons of languid faith: "In such and such circumstances I had recourse to the intercession of the Holy Souls in Purgatory, and they have never yet failed me!"

Daily does the Angel of Death enter our homes and summon from us those that are rooted in our affections, and for whom our hearts feel love and esteem. Daily must we bow our heads in reverent silence and submission to the decree that snatches from us some loved one. Perhaps it is a wife who mourns the loss of her husband. She finds comfort and companionship in praying for the repose of his soul; in the words of Tertullian, "she prays for his soul, and begs for him in the interim refreshments, and in the first resurrection companionship, and maketh offerings on the anniversary day of his falling asleep." Perhaps it is a husband whose loving wife has gone to sleep in death. Then will he hold her memory sacred, and offer thereto the incense of unceasing prayer, so that it may be said of him, as St. Jerome wrote to Pammachius: "Thou hast rendered what was due to each part, giving tears to the body and alms to the soul. . . . There were thy tears where thou knewest was death, there were thy works where thou knewest was life. . . . Already is she honored with thy merits; already is she fed with thy bread and abounds with thy riches."

Perhaps it is a dear friend around whom our heartstrings were entwined, and whose love for us was more than we were worthy of; whose counsels were our guide; whose soul was an open book in which we daily read the lesson of high resolve and sincere purpose; whose virtuous life was a continuous aspiration urging us on to noble thought and noble deed. And yet our friendship may have bound his soul in ties too earthly, and retarded his progress in perfection; in consequence he may still dread the light of God's countenance, and may be lingering in this state of purgation. It behoves us in all earnestness and in friendship's sacred claim to pray unceasingly for that friend, beseeching God to let the dews of Divine mercy fall upon his parching soul, assuage his pain, and, taking him to Himself, complete his happiness.

So the sacred duty of prayer for the dead runs through all the relations of life. From all comes the cry begging for our prayers. Every reminder that we receive is a voice from the grave. Now it is the mention of a name that once brought gladness to our hearts; or we come across a letter written by a hand whose grasp used to thrill our souls—that hand now stiffened and cold in death; or it is the sight of some relic that vividly recalls the dear one passed away; or it is a dream—and to whom has not such a dream occurred?—in which we live over again the pleasant past with the bosom friend of our soul, and he is back once more in the flesh, re-enacting the scenes of former days, breathing and talking as naturally as though there were no break in his life or ours, and we had never parted. When we awaken from our dream, and the pang of reality, like a keen blade, penetrates our hearts, let us not rest content with a vain sigh of regret or with useless tears of grief; let us pray God to give the departed soul eternal rest and admit it to the perpetual light of His presence. And in like manner should we regard all other reminders as so many appeals to the charity of our prayers. In this way will the keeping of the memory of those gone before us be to them a blessing and to us a consolation.

—BROTHER AZARIAS in *The Ave Maria**

We read in the *Life of St. Gertrude* that on one occasion a person was told in her presence that a relative had died who had not led a very good life. The Saint was so moved by her friend's affliction that she offered to pray for the soul of the deceased. Our Lord taught her that the information had been given in her presence by a special arrangement of His providence. She said: "Lord, couldst not Thou have given me the compassion without this?" He answered: "I take partic-ular pleasure in prayers for the dead when they are addressed to Me from natural compassion united to a good will; thus a good work becomes perfected." When St. Gertrude had prayed for this soul a long time, he appeared to her under a horrible form, as if blackened by fire and con-torted with pain. She saw no one near him; but his sins, which he had not fully expiated, were his executioners, and each member suffered for the sins to which it had been accessory.

Then St. Gertrude, desiring to intercede with her Spouse for him, said lovingly: "My Lord, wilt Thou not relieve this

---

* Copied by kind permission of the Editor.

soul for my sake?" He replied: "Not only would I deliver this soul, but many souls, for your love. How do you wish Me to show him mercy? Shall I release him at once from all his sufferings?"

"Perhaps, Lord," she said, "this would be contrary to the decrees of Thy justice." He answered: "It would not be contrary to it if you asked Me with faith, for, as I foresee the future, I prepared him for this when in his agony." She then said: "I beseech of Thee, Salvation of my soul, to perfect this work according to Thy mercy, in which I have the most perfect confidence." When she had said this, the soul appeared under a human form and in great joy, but still bearing some marks of his former sins; however, the Saint knew that he must be purified further and made white as snow before he would be fit to enter into the Divine Presence; and to effect this it was necessary for him to suffer as if from the blows of an iron hammer. Furthermore, he had continued so long in sin that the process of cleansing his soul was much prolonged, and he also suffered as if exposed for a year to the rays of a scorching sun.

As the Saint wondered at this, she was instructed that those who have committed many and grievous sins are not assisted by the ordinary suffrages of the Church until they are partly purified by Divine Justice; and that they cannot avail of the prayers of the faithful, which are constantly descending on the souls in Purgatory like a gentle and refreshing dew, or like a sweet and soothing ointment. St. Gertrude said to Our Lord: "O my most loving Lord! Tell me, I beseech Thee, what work or prayers will most easily obtain mercy from Thee for those sinners who have died in a state of grace, so that they may be delivered from this terrible impediment which prevents them from obtaining the benefit of the prayers of the Church. For this soul appears to me now, when relieved from this burden, as if it had ascended from Hell to Heaven." Our Lord replied: "The only way to obtain such a favor is Divine love; neither prayers nor any other good works will avail without this, and it must be such a love as you now have for Me; and as none can have this grace unless I bestow it, so also none can obtain these advantages after death unless I have prepared them for it by some special grace during life. Know, however, that the prayers and good works of the faithful relieve souls gradually from this heavy burden, and that they are delivered sooner or later according to the fervor and pure intentions of those who thus serve them, and according to the merit which they have acquired for themselves during their mortal life."

Then the soul for whom St. Gertrude had prayed besought Our Lord, by the love which had brought Him down from Heaven to die upon the Cross, to reward abundantly those who prayed for him; and Our Lord appeared to take a piece of gold from him and lay it by to recompense those who had assisted him by their prayers.

—Life of St. Gertrude

✎ SEVENTH DAY ✎

A Day of Prayer for Poor Souls Who Have None to Pray for Them

"**A**S you measure to others," says our Blessed Saviour, "it shall be measured to you again." Now, what would you wish to be done for you if in Purgatory? Surely you would not like to be forgotten—to have no longer a share in the prayers of the faithful. To escape so great a misery, which is often an effect of Divine Justice on such as have had no charity for the deceased, be very earnest today in your supplications for those Poor Souls who have none to pray for them.

———

The duty of helping the poor sufferers in Purgatory by our prayers is a great and holy act of charity which is very dear to the Sacred Heart of Jesus, but which is by very many altogether unheeded, and by very few performed with that earnest, untiring perseverance which it so well deserves. Is there one of us who, passing on any errand of business or pleasure, could see a fellow creature in fearful agony, from which, by a little delay, a little extra trouble, we might liberate him, or at least assuage and shorten his torment, and yet would pass on without turning, without speaking one compassionate word? Not one of us, surely. Yet daily and hourly, as we pass on our errands of duty and pleasure, there are innumerable multitudes of our fellow creatures calling to us from wide oceans of unimaginable and undying fire; and the dew of charity seems dried up in our hearts, and we have none to give them. Daily and hourly they are stretching their manacled hands toward us, praying for one touch of the talismanic power of indulgenced prayer to lighten the weight, to send ringing downward the chains that bind them; and we lock up the rich treasure before their pleading eyes, and turn away!

We turn away because we cannot spare the time from our amusements, our dress, from the thousand and one things that make up the business of our lives. Daily and hourly they plead to us who think that we love Jesus to consider how they have seen Him, and know what He is, while we only guess, imploring of us to use our power with their Sovereign to shorten their time of banishment, to rid them of their keenest pang—separation from Him. They have seen Him, and their souls are straining after Him, and their hearts are thirsting for Him, with a straining and a thirsting that only immortality could bear and live. We stand by, and hearken not, and our precious power is lost, lies utterly useless; and are we the dearer to the Heart of Jesus for it?

Oh! Are we deaf, that their voices are unanswered? Are our hearts turned to stone, that human souls can thus cry to us in vain? We have heard their cry, oh! so often: *"Have pity on us! Have pity on us, at least you, our friends!"* Passing by a quiet graveyard in the calm of a summer evening, we have heard it. It has floated on the faint breath of summer air, stealing over the peaceful green mounds; in the light rustle of the drooping trees; in the softened murmur of the little brook, slipping between the graves. It has trembled over the whole scene. Oh, the gentle, holy resignation, the perfect humility of that cry, *"Have pity!"* We have heard it rising above the measured fall of footsteps, above the muffled roll of carriage wheels, above all the stately pomp of each well-appointed funeral. *"Have pity!* This is not what we want; what care we for all this pomp and show? It is of no value here. Oh, the unutterable value of one 'My Jesus, mercy!' The priceless worth of one fervent 'Hail Mary!' And you waste your time thus. Have you no love as well as respect for our memory?"

We have heard this cry, strong and eager, coming through the twilight aisles of the silent chapel as we knelt in prayer: *"Have pity on us!* Speak for us there, at the Master's feet. *You* are happy, feeling Him so near, almost hearing His voice in the quiet, holy stillness. *We* are chained down in exquisite torment; we stretch our hands toward Him, we strain our eyes after Him, but we cannot see Him, we cannot feel Him near. You feel your soul filled with gentle, holy thoughts, and a feeling of deep peace; we are surrounded by surging waves of liquid fire, and there is no peace for us, save that we suffer for His love. *Have pity on us!* You are trying to come near to Him; you are always trying to think what it will be to be loosed from earth and to fly away to Him, your Lord, your Beloved, your only Rest. But you cannot; the vision of His Face floats away just when you think you can almost see it, and leaves your soul dark again. And ah! Now, more than ever have pity; for we have seen Him. We have known what it is to be released and to dart up to Him, attracted by a magnetism unknown to you on earth. We have seen His Face, that beautiful Face, that is always rising up in your soul; but it is so indistinct, you cannot imagine it. You have not felt the intense and overwhelming love of Him that taught us to fly with joy into these very flames in which we now languish, in the hope of becoming a little less unworthy of His love. You cannot picture the longing to be again with Him that makes every moment a tedious age. You do not know it, or you would not be so chary of each little prayer that wins for us the striking off of one hundred or more of those dragging centuries that you call days. Oh, *have pity on us*—speak for us!"

It is more than merely a work of charity, and the most perfect of all works of fraternal charity. It is besides a work of self-interest. Let us go back to my first example—the person who, passing on a work of duty or pleasure, refuses to pause in order to aid a suffering fellow creature. Suppose that by releasing that sufferer he could restore him to a high and confidential post in the court of some mighty Sovereign where he would use his utmost power in behalf of his benefactor, all his energy quickened and made earnest in the strength of the deepest gratitude for the service done him, would you not think him mad who passed on and turned not to aid him, and let the golden opportunity go by for ever? It is but another instance of the indifference we show for the things of Heaven, while we strive earnestly after the things of earth.

Think of the gratitude of that glorious spirit, mounting from the crucible of Purgatory, shining and perfect, the debt which it owed to a just and infinitely loving Maker paid to the last farthing. How was it paid? By that plenary indulgence that you threw your whole soul into winning for it; by the unaccountable merits of that Holy Sacrifice offered to wash away the stains that yet marred the exquisite beauty of that spirit, and made it yet unfit for Heaven's perfection; nay, perhaps by the little prayer of one or three hundred days' indulgence that only cost you one short sentence breathed to Heaven from your heart's core, but which paid the balance of the debt, which otherwise must be told down by that soul in pain and anguish. Think of it speeding upward into the very bosom of God, perfect at last, and worthy of Him. Perfect! And is not gratitude a grand, rich attribute of perfection? Yes, and not one new glory is added, not one speechless joy won at last, but that soul will think of how a heart had pleaded bravely for it on the earth that looks so cold and dark beyond the brightness of Heaven.

Never can that heart, still bound to that cold earth, be tempted, or sad, or tried; never can it cry to Heaven for help without that glorious spirit casting itself before the throne of God, crying with all the gratitude of its heavenly perfection for the benefactor who paid the debt which bound it in a fiery prison, far from God and Heaven; paying back the loan a hundred and a thousandfold.

High and favored in the court of the Sovereign are those weary ones who called to us in the solemn stillness of the little graveyard in that bright summer sunset a little while ago. Sweet and strong amid the shining bands of the King's angelic minstrels is that wailing voice that rose above the sound of useless pomp in that gorgeous funeral that men called honorable. Unutterable the joy that bows down the soul, and unutterable the beauty that gladdens the eyes of those whose eager, half-impatient voices came to us, through the Church's twilight aisles, that night when we knelt in close converse with our sacramental Lord. Are we not well repaid that from those shining thrones, from that choir of heavenly minstrels, from those bending forms, a prayer is rising for us, because we stole those five minutes from our pleasures, because we gave that little alms that we could only pretty well spare, because we hearkened and did breathe a prayer to Jesus in the quiet stillness of the Church that evening, because we went that once or twice round the holy Stations of the Cross and offered it for them, because we paused that once or twice and breathed that little indulgenced prayer, that *De Profundis*, with our whole hearts, and then went our way again? Are we not well repaid? —J. M. M.

The venerable Sister Paula of St. Teresa was a Dominican nun of the Convent of St. Catherine in Naples. One day, being in prayer, she was transported in spirit to Purgatory, where she saw a great number of souls plunged in flames. Close to them she saw Our Divine Lord, attended by His Angels, who pointed out, one after the other, several souls that He desired to take to Heaven, whither they ascended in transports of delight. At this sight the servant of God, addressing herself to her Divine Spouse, said to Him: "O my beloved Lord, why this choice among such a vast multitude?" "I have released," He deigned to reply, "those who during life performed great acts of charity and mercy, and who have merited that I should fulfill My promise in their regard, *Blessed are the merciful, for they shall obtain mercy.*"

When one earnestly wishes to obtain a favor from God through the intercession of the Blessed Virgin, or one of the Saints, it is usual to say: "If this favor be granted, I will make such and such an offering, or give such an alms." Far preferable and more efficacious would it prove to give beforehand what we intend to offer in thanksgiving; for thus, by our confidence, we oblige, as it were, Almighty God, Our Blessed Lady and the Saints to listen favorably and to grant our petitions. We also fulfill the precept of Christ: "Give, and it shall be given to you." Our Divine Lord does not say, "Promise to give, and you shall receive," but, "Give first, and then you shall receive."　　　—ST. JOHN BOSCO

✎ EIGHTH DAY ✎

A Day of Prayer for the Souls in Purgatory Who during Life Were Most Devoted To the Blessed Sacrament

IT is no small aggravation to the sufferings of those souls in Purgatory who were most devoted to the Blessed Sacrament during life to be no longer able to receive that Divine Food which is the Paradise of the earth; to be no longer capable of speaking heart to heart to Jesus in His holy Sacrament, or contemplate under the mystic veil that Divine Countenance on which the Angels delight to gaze. In recompense for their devotion and to hasten the possession of their Sovereign Good, offer for them a fervent Communion.

The suffering of sense in Purgatory is caused by the awful flames into which the soul is cast, and which are like to the flames of Hell, as St. Thomas tells us, save in their duration; and that in Purgatory they burn to cleanse, while in Hell they burn without purifying. If the material body suffers excruciating torments when exposed to the action of a small flame, who can conceive what the spiritual soul, untrammelled by flesh, must suffer when enveloped by a fire created by the justice of God to purify it?

We sometimes speak lightly enough of Purgatory and perhaps even reconcile ourselves with a certain degree of contentment to the prospect of having to spend a time amidst its sufferings, encouraging ourselves with the thought that, once there, Heaven will be certainly ours, sooner or later; and depending on this assurance, we satisfy ourselves with a low standard of virtue—such, perhaps, as would barely save us from eternal sufferings. But in all this we betray our thoughtlessness, and show a lightness of disposition which seems incapable of grasping the extent of an evil simply because it is not present to us. When the reality comes upon us we shall assuredly have far other thoughts. Anyway, we know—whether we take time to dwell upon the truth or not—that in Purgatory there is intense suffering, and that those who are tormented there appeal to us silently but powerfully. Perhaps among them may be someone very dear to us—it may be a fond parent, a devoted brother or sister, or a beloved child; and can we, if we are not altogether insensible, be indifferent to their pleading: *"Miseremini mei! Miseremini mei saltem vos amici mei!"* (Have pity on me! Have pity on me, at least you, my friends). Surely, unless we are utterly devoid of sympathy, we cannot resist such a touching appeal.

THE CRY OF THE SUFFERING SOULS

Out of the sea of encircling fire,
Out of the fetters of torturing flame—
Glowing with ceaseless, insatiate desire,
The cry of their need mounting higher and higher,
Ever they call to us, ever the same:
          "Miseremini mei! Miseremini mei!"

Loved ones are there—ay, the lost ones we tended,
Wiping the death-dews from lip and from brow;
Friends whom we cherished and foes we befriended,
Foeman and friend in the hot surges blended—
Hark! how their voices appeal to us now:
          "Miseremini mei! Miseremini mei!"

"At least you, my dear ones, have pity upon us!"
(The cry of each soul doth its mourners pursue),
"The hand of the Lord presses heavily on us;
And oh! by the kindness you often have shown us,
By the love of the by-gone, so tender and true,
          "Miseremini mei! Miseremini mei!"

"We were comrades of old: oft the teardrop hath started
To dim your bright eyes at the sound of our names,
Yet ye scarce breathed a prayer when our spirits departed,
For ye deemed us in Paradise, glad and pure-hearted,
Whilst we languished forlorn, in this prison of flames.
          "Miseremini mei! Miseremini mei!"

"We were Pontiffs and Bishops—yea, priests, nuns and friars;
Though holy our lives—ah! the judgment was stern.
The purest of gold are the heavenly lyres
Which ring thro' the halls of the Ransomed. These fires
Are purging our gold from its dross as we burn;
          "Miseremini mei! Miseremini mei!"

"Oh, stretch forth your hands to our help, we beseech you!
Offer Mass, offer alms, offer penance severe;
If, out of these fetters, our spirits could reach you,
How soon the sad sight of our suff'rings would teach you
Dread lessons of mercy and holiest fear!
        "Miseremini mei! Miseremini mei!"

"For life and its loves had so much to distract us.
Joy sat at the banquet, with Beauty and Wit;
But when to these realms God's justice had tracked us,
Alas! how the scourges of Memory racked us
For sins that we once deemed it sport to commit!
        "Miseremini mei! Miseremini mei!"

"Oh, pray for us, plead for us! soon shall ye follow us;
And, if your suffrages win us release,
Happy with God, in His Paradise glorious,
We shall be advocates, mighty, victorious,
To speed your glad souls to those mansions of peace.
        "Miseremini mei! Miseremini mei!"

Thus, and forever, from out the fierce embers,
Ringeth to Heaven that chorus of pain!
(Wistfully wailing, like winds of November),
Waiting their advent, their dawn in December,
Spouses of Christ are they—Christians, remember!
Say, in Christ's Name, shall they pray us in vain?—
        "Miseremini mei! Miseremini mei!"
                                —ELEANOR DONNELLY

Saint Margaret Mary being one day in prayer before the
Blessed Sacrament, a person all on fire suddenly appeared
before her, whose burning heat penetrated her so powerfully that she thought herself consumed with the same fire.
She did not recognize the person, but his state caused her
to shed many tears. The suffering soul then told her that he
was a Benedictine monk who a short time before had been
Prior of the Convent of Paray, to whom she had once con-

fessed, and who had given her some consolation on that occasion by allowing her to receive Holy Communion. In his sufferings God had permitted him to address himself to Saint Margaret Mary, that he might obtain relief by her prayers. He requested that she would offer for him and apply to him all that she should do and suffer for the space of three months.

He then made known to her three reasons for the great suffering to which he was condemned. The first was that he had been too much attached to his reputation, which had sometimes made him prefer his interest on this point to the glory of God. The second was his want of charity towards his brethren. The third was a certain too natural affection he had had for creatures, and the testimonies he had given them of it in the spiritual conversations he had had with them, "which," said he, "much displeased God."

Saint Margaret Mary promised that if she could obtain permission she would perform what he requested. It was granted, but her promise did not deliver her from the sight of this afflicting spectacle, which never left her during all that time. She seemed incessantly to see this religious near her, who communicated his flames to the side on which he appeared to remain, and in all this half of her body she felt such intense pain that she wept almost continually. Her superior, who knew her state and the cause of her pain, found that nothing gave her any alleviation but prescribing her penances, which holy practices appeared to give some relief both to the religious and the sister. At the end of three months they were both delivered from their sufferings, for Saint Margaret Mary saw the holy religious ascend to Heaven filled with joy, after having testified his gratitude and assured her that he would protect her before God.

∽ NINTH DAY ∽

A Day of Prayer for the Souls in Purgatory Who during Life Were Most Devoted To Our Blessed Lady

MARY, from her nearness to Jesus, has imbibed many traits of His Sacred Heart. She shares in a pre-eminent degree His Divine compassion for sorrow and suffering. Where He loves and pities, she also loves and pities. Nay, may we not well say that all enduring anguish of soul and writhing under the pangs of a lacerated heart are especially dear to both Jesus and His Mother? Was not Jesus the Man of Sorrows? and did He not constitute Mary the Mother of suffering and sorrowing humanity? And even as His Divine breast knew keenest sorrow, did not a sword of sorrow pierce her soul? She participated in the Agony of Jesus only as such a Mother can share the agony of such a Son; in the tenderest manner, therefore, does she commiserate sorrow and suffering wherever found. Though now far beyond all touch of pain and misery, still, as the devoted Mother of a pain-stricken race, she continues to watch, to shield, to aid, and to strengthen her children in their wrestlings with these mysterious visitants.

Nor does Our Lady's interest cease upon this side of the grave. It accompanies souls beyond. And when she beholds those souls undergoing their final purgation before entering upon the enjoyment of the Beatific Vision, she pities them with a pity all the more heartfelt because their suffering is so much greater than any they could have endured in this life. See the state of these souls. They are in grace and favor with God; they are burning with love for Him; they are yearning with a yearning boundless in its intensity to drink refreshment of life and love and sanctification, and to be replenished with goodness and truth, and to perfect their nature at the fountainhead of all truth, all goodness, all love, and all perfection. They are yearning; but so clearly and piercingly does the white light of God's truth and God's holiness shine through them, and penetrate every fold and recess of their moral nature, and reveal to them every slightest imperfection, that they dare not approach Him and gratify their intense desire to be united with Him.

Of the nature and intensity of the sufferings of souls undergoing this purification, we on earth can form but the faintest conception. Not so Our Blessed Lady. She sees things as they are. She sees the great love animating those Holy Souls. She sees their great desire to be united to God, the sole center and object of their being. She sees and appreciates the struggle going on in them between that intense desire, that great yearning, that unfilled and unsatiated vagueness arising from their privation of the only fullness that could replenish them, on the one hand; and, on the other, the sense of their unfitness—keen, strong, deep, intense, overwhelming them and driving them back to the flames of pain until they shall have satisfied God's justice to the last farthing, and every slightest stain has been cleansed, and they stand forth in the light of God's sanctity whole and spotless. She sees the terrible struggle, and her Heart goes out in tender pity to these her children, washed and ransomed by the Blood of Christ, and she is well disposed to extend to them the aid of her powerful intercession. She is fitly called the Mother of Mercy. Her merciful Heart goes out to these, the favored ones of her Son, all the more lovingly because they are unable to help themselves.

—BROTHER AZARIAS

From the following example we learn how Our Lord hastens to deliver from Purgatory souls who during life honored His Blessed Mother.

In the Book of her *Foundations*, St. Teresa tells us that Don Bernardino di Mendoza gave her a house, garden and vineyard, which he owned near Valladolid, that she might establish there a convent in honor of the holy Mother of God. Two months after this, and before the foundation was effected, he was suddenly taken ill and lost the power of speech, so that he could not make a confession, though he gave many signs of contrition. "He died," says St. Teresa, "far from the place where I then was. But Our Lord spoke to me, and told me that he was saved, though he had run a great risk, for that He had had mercy on him because of the gift he had given for the convent of His Blessed Mother, but that his soul would not be freed from Purgatory until the first Mass was said in the new house. I felt so deeply the pains this soul was suffering that although I was very desirous of accomplishing the foundation of Toledo, I left it at once for Valladolid.

"Praying one day at Medina del Campo, Our Lord told me to make haste, for that soul was suffering grievously. On this I started at once, thought I was not well prepared for it, and arrived at Valladolid on St. Laurence's Day." She then goes on to relate that as the new building was very extensive and would take a considerable time before completion, she had a temporary chapel prepared for the accommodation of the Sisters whom she had brought with her. She deeply regretted her inability to build at once the permanent church, as she feared that until that was done Don Bernardino should be detained in Purgatory; but how great was her consolation when, as the first Mass was being offered in this chapel, she saw in an ecstasy the soul of her generous benefactor ascend to Heaven. Rejoicing at his happiness, she thanked Our Lord for the solicitude with which He had hastened to deliver him, and became from that time more devoted than ever to the souls in Purgatory as she perceived the great interest taken in them by Our Lord.

November should be a month for compensations. The debt of love which we neglected to pay to relatives and friends while they lived with us on earth we may now discharge, and with generous interest. For the tender sympathy, the loving smile, the kindly word, the helping hand, which we once refused, we may now substitute the fervent ejaculatory prayer, the attendance at Mass, the recitation of the Rosary, or the Stations of the Cross. To atone for the undue rigor of our treatment of many of the faithful departed, we may now gain and apply to them innumerable indulgences, partial and plenary. For those suffering souls who have the strongest claims on our affection or our justice we should, as far as it is in our power to do so, secure the offering up of the adorable and propitiatory Sacrifice of the Altar. If it is always "a holy and wholesome thought to pray for the dead, that they may be loosed from their sins," (*2 Machabees* 12:46), it is especially during the present month that Catholic charity yields prompt and generous response to the pleading cry that Purgatory is ever sending up to earth: "Have pity on me! Have pity on me, at least you, my friends; for the hand of the Lord hath touched me!"

—*Ave Maria*

⤳ TENTH DAY ⤳

A Day of Prayer for the Souls in Purgatory Who during Life Were Most Devoted to St. Joseph

IF we reflect on the close alliance St. Joseph has with the Incarnate Word and His Immaculate Mother, we must surely acknowledge him worthy of our deepest love and veneration. One of the best modes of honoring him is to supplicate the Most High for souls who were devoted to him during life and are now suffering in Purgatory.

St. Joseph may be regarded as the special Patron of Purgatory because he is, after Our Blessed Lady, the most powerful and charitable of all the Saints. The Prime Minister of Egypt had authority to open or shut the gates of the prison at will, which has always been considered a privilege of the highest order. Thus it is with St. Joseph, of whom the first Joseph was a true type. Assured of the power of our holy Patriarch, can we doubt his goodwill? Who can express his

Almighty, eternal, just and merciful God,
Give to us miserable ones the grace to do for You alone
what we know You want us to do
and always to desire what pleases You.
Inwardly cleansed, interiorly enlightened,
and inflamed by the fire of the Holy Spirit,
May we be able to follow in the footprints of Your
beloved Son, our Lord Jesus Christ,
And by Your grace alone, may we make our way to You.
Most High, Who live and rule
in perfect Trinity and simple Unity,
And are glorified God almighty,
forever and ever.
Amen

Our Retreat House Offers:

- Beautiful Chapel
- Library
- Conference room
- Gift Shop
- Spiritual Direction
- Confession
- Four Conferences
- Outdoor Stations of the Cross; Walking Crown Rosary

burning zeal in favor of the poor sufferers in Purgatory, who are in his eyes all-beautiful by Sanctifying Grace, beloved by God, and destined soon to enjoy the Beatific Vision in the realms of bliss? St. Joseph, before entering into Heaven, passed through Limbo, which, doubtless, was not a place of torments like Purgatory; still, it was not Heaven. Here eager souls sighed for the coming of the Messias, and saluted Him from afar. This great Saint mingled his desires with theirs. In consoling the souls in Purgatory, St. Joseph continues the merciful avocation Divine Providence assigned him in Limbo.

It is acknowledged that the Saints have in Heaven a particular power to perpetuate the mission exercised by them on earth. Therefore the Church implores of certain Saints, recognized as mediators of peace, to avert impending horrors of war, and of others to obtain graces analogous to those which they had procured for their neighbor during life. St. Joseph having been destined by God to bring consolation to the souls in Limbo, he, like a beautiful aurora, dissipated the darkness of night by announcing to them their approaching deliverance. With what joy must they not have greeted his arrival! Each one came to him to hear of the long-wished-for Messias. Adam and Eve wished to learn particulars regarding her who had been announced to them as destined to crush the serpent's head. Abel wished to know Him whose Blood cried to Heaven for mercy more eloquently than his for vengeance. Abraham exulted with joy at the thought of seeing Him whom he had so long yearned to behold. Joseph listened with rapture to the Saint whose name he bore, and of whom he had been a figure. The prophets were in ecstasy at the realization of their inspired prophecies. St. Joseph related to them the marvels of which he had been the witness and co-operator. Who more capable of speaking of Our Blessed Lord and His holy Mother than he who had had the happiness of sharing in their dolors and joys for thirty years—he who so often carried in his arms and pressed to his heart the Desire of all Nations—in a word, he whom the God Incarnate called Father, and obeyed with filial affection, and whom Mary, Queen of Angels and Saints, and Mother of God, revered as her chaste spouse?

The beautiful mission of Consoler of the Dead is too glorious, too dear to God and to the Saints, not to have it still continued to St. Joseph after the Ascension of Our Divine Redeemer. A venerable writer says that the Son of God, having the keys of Paradise, has given one to His Immaculate Mother and the other to St. Joseph. Oh, then, you who so much love the dear departed ones, you who still weep at the remembrance of a cherished parent, a beloved brother or sister or dear friend, have recourse to St. Joseph! You who dread the flames of Purgatory, invoke St. Joseph, for though he is the mediator of all who are detained in those cleansing fires, he exercises special influence in behalf of persons who during life have been distinguished for their zeal in honoring him. Lastly, after the example of St. Joseph, let us be messengers of joy to those helpless souls detained captive in the fiery prison by offering fervent prayers and gaining indulgences for their relief.

———————

Sister Marie de St. Pierre, Carmelite of Tours, was very much devoted to praying for the Poor Souls in Purgatory. One of them seems to have especially claimed the spiritual alms of her holy prayers. In reading the following account given by herself, we cannot fail to be edified by the tender, holy ardor with which she devoted her prayers and penances to the relief of those departed souls who seemed in greatest need of them.

The sudden and frightful death of the Duke of Orleans, eldest son and presumptive heir of King Louis Philippe, had just cast a deep gloom over all France. A spirited horse attached to his carriage having run off, the Duke was thrown out, and dashed against the ground with such violence that he died almost instantly. The news spread like wildfire, and even penetrated the precincts of Carmel of Tours. Everywhere it made a profound impression, especially as the Duke had some years previously, in spite of the remonstrances of the Archbishop of Paris, and to the great scandal of Catholics, married a Protestant princess. For this reason many persons were inclined to regard his death as a chastisement from Heaven.

"One Sunday," writes the Sister, "I was making my usual mental prayer. No thoughts of the Duke of Orleans were in my mind. I had, indeed, heard vaguely of the accident, but had never dreamed of praying for this poor prince since his death, when suddenly the memory of him came vividly before me. During the recitation of the Little Hours of the Divine Office, I was most profoundly impressed with the feeling that his soul was suffering in Purgatory and needed succor. It seemed to me that the nearer I approached the Divine Heart of Jesus the deeper became my emotion, and my utterance was at last so choked by tears that I could with great difficulty recite the Office in choir. I felt myself most strongly attracted to this suffering soul, whom Our Lord desired to deliver from the flames. Having received Holy Communion for him, Jesus inspired me to offer to His Eternal Father for this intention all His infinite merits. During my thanksgiving it seemed to me that my soul met his in Our Lord, and I then said to him: 'Poor Prince! What now remains to you of the world's grandeur and riches? Behold, you are today glad indeed to receive the benefit of a humble Carmelite's Holy Communion! Remember me when you enter Heaven.' Our Lord urged me to pray for him, and with such extraordinary charity, that it was even greater than had ever moved me for my nearest relatives. He suggested to me to offer for this soul's relief all He had suffered when crowned with thorns and ridiculed as a mock King; and before a picture representing this stage of His sacred Passion, I passed the rest of the morning praying for the Prince. Three times that day I recited in the presence of the Blessed Sacrament the six *Paters, Aves* and *Glorias* to gain the numberless plenary and partial indulgences attached to these prayers in connection with the Blue Scapular, and which are applicable to the dead. Next morning, Monday, I was again inspired to receive Holy Communion for the same intention. This suffering soul seemed inseparably attached to mine, accompanying it everywhere; and all the acts of mortification I performed were for its repose."

On the 20th of March the Sister writes thus to the Mother Prioress:

"As I have reached the end of the fortnight during which you allowed me to abandon myself into Our Lord's hands to suffer whatever He judged proper, making an offering of it in behalf of the suffering soul in Purgatory now absorbing my attention, permit me to give you an account of all that has taken place in my soul from the 26th of February to the 19th of March.

"I will say in all simplicity that my soul felt for this poor prince a tenderness akin to that which urges a mother to be ever seeking remedies for a sick child. Day and night have my thoughts been occupied with the alleviation of his sufferings. At last I asked my holy Guardian Angel never to let me lose sight of him until he had entered Heaven, and I believe he has charitably granted my request, for supernatural feelings have incessantly prompted me to offer all my actions for his deliverance. Every Communion—except one, which duty required me to give a departed Sister—all the prayers I recited, the Holy Sacrifice of the Mass, many times the Stations of the Cross, the penances you have allowed me to perform, were the suffrages I had the consolation of presenting to God in behalf of this soul. Though you have seen my face swollen, I must say that my corporal sufferings were slight, and I was deeply grieved that they were; it was upon my soul Our Lord imprinted the seal of suffering. To that sweet union and interior peace I had enjoyed succeeded a terrible storm. Our Lord hid Himself, making me thus feel most keenly my misery and unworthiness. Darkness indeed followed light; yet, though the Divine Master was striking me with one hand, He sustained me with the other and gave me courage to say to Him: 'My God, only preserve me from offending Thee herein, and willingly do I accept these trials, that through them this poor soul may the sooner enter into bliss, and glorify Thee for me. Behold, Lord, this is all I desire!'

"The feast of our holy father St. Joseph was approaching. I made a novena in preparation for this great solemnity, supplicating the glorious Saint to obtain of God thereon this soul's deliverance, and promising to continue the penances I had been permitted to perform. On the eve of the feast my emotion was almost overpowering through the ardor of my desire. I was in inexpressible torment. I could scarcely take my food, and with difficulty could I restrain my tears; my soul was wounded, but truly by a sentiment wholly supernatural, for I had not even known the Prince. Ah! If ever I felt the privation my vow of poverty imposes, it was then, for most assuredly any little funds in my possession would have been appropriated to Masses for him; but a consoling thought came to mind. I said to myself: 'Everything have I given to my Heavenly Spouse, consequently, He has reciprocally given Himself to me; hence His goods are mine.' Then, full of confidence, I offered the Eternal Father all the treasures of His Divine Son to supply the deficiencies of my poverty, and I united my intention with that of every priest who was celebrating the Holy Sacrifice of the Mass.

'Next day, the 19th of March, Our Lord made me understand that I must still continue my charity in behalf of this suffering soul by offering for him the Holy Communion I was about to receive, and thus gain for him the indulgence applicable to the dead. I assented to this somewhat reluctantly, for on this great Feast of our Holy Order I had intended applying to my own soul, my own especial needs, the benefit of the indulgence; but since Our Lord wished otherwise I submitted to His holy Will, and did as He had inspired me, interceding for the Prince with all the powers of my soul and all the affections of my heart.

"Since that day, Reverend Mother, I am no longer troubled; the burden seems lifted from me, and I can say no prayers for him except the *Laudate*. Hence I believe that my feeble services, united with the fervent prayers of our sisters, have relieved him. The most Blessed Virgin has doubtless obtained his salvation, and our glorious father St. Joseph his entrance into Heaven, for I hope, and my soul has the interior confidence, that on the feast of this great Saint he was delivered from Purgatory. God, however, has given me no supernatural assurance of this. I adore His designs without wishing to penetrate them, for I am most unworthy of such a grace. The Prince, as is well known, died very suddenly by a terrible accident, and without the consoling aids of our holy religion; but an act of sincere contrition may have obtained his salvation, the mercy of God surpassing all His works."

Three years later it was revealed to Sister St. Pierre that this soul, the object of such fervent prayers, had been delivered from Purgatory. On the 26th of April, 1846, she writes thus:

"After Holy Communion Our Lord said to me: 'Allow thyself to follow the inspirations of grace.' I obeyed, and this Divine Saviour began to manifest Himself to me. But oh, what shall I now say! O infinite goodness of my God, assist me to speak in order that the knowledge and love of Thee may be thereby increased upon earth! Suddenly Our Lord said to me: 'Behold him for whom you so fervently prayed. I bring him to you that he may thank you for all your charity toward his soul. Behold the excess of My mercy in his regard. Had I left him on earth, he would have enjoyed the ambition of encircling his brow with a perishable, earthly crown, while now in Heaven I have given him an immortal crown of glory.' I beheld by an intellectual vision this soul at the side of Jesus; and as he turned toward me I said: 'Ah, it is Our Lord you must thank, for I am nothing. It was His merits I offered to God.' The soul then replied: "When brought before the judgment seat of God, I was covered with the infinite merits of Jesus Christ. It is to the Blessed Virgin I owe my salvation, and to St. Joseph's assistance my deliverance from Purgatory.'

"'O most happy soul!' I said, 'pray for France—pray for me!' And in a transport of gratitude at the thought of God's infinite mercy I repeated: 'Happy soul, pray for me!

Together let us prostrate ourselves at the feet of Our Lord Jesus Christ; aid me to render Him worthy homage.' Our Lord then said to me: 'Now this soul will pray for you.' And I repeated: 'Pray for me! But how,' I asked, 'shall I henceforth invoke you?' The soul answered: 'My name is Ferdinand. Call me Ferdinand. I assure you I was called Ferdinand.' It seemed to me that he repeated his name several times, as if to prove thereby the truth of what I saw, for I did not know the Prince's name. He added: 'I reign now with Jesus Christ; I am crowned in Heaven.' I continued: 'God's goodness is very great, I know, yet I did not dare to think you had already entered into eternal glory; but now I perceive that this was through a special act of Divine mercy.' I was touched to the very depths at all that I saw, heard, and understood. The excess of Divine charity toward this soul filled me with joy. At this moment the 'turn-bell'* rang, and I left Our Lord in obedience to the call of duty. Desirous of assuring myself that what had just taken place was not an illusion, I asked one of the sisters whom I met, and who must know the name of the aforesaid Prince, what it was. 'He was called Ferdinand,' she replied. This answer produced a strong impression on me, stamping as it did the seal of truth upon what I had just experienced. Moreover, the Divine operation in my soul on this occasion was of the strongest kind."

NOTE.—Although this event is connected with the political questions of the past, we have thought proper to give it in detail, not even withholding the real names. The pure intention of our holy Carmelite will justify us in the eyes of our readers for having done so. Moreover, the incident contains a consoling reflection which should escape the observation of no one—that in the most distressing accidents of life, seemingly chastisements of Divine Justice upon families and empires, there is often for the salvation of individuals an unsuspected merciful side which proves the infinite goodness of God and the admirable workings of His Provi-

---

* Sister St. Pierre fulfilled the office of portress in her convent.

dence. This communication was laid before Monseigneur Morlot. The prelate was so fully impressed with the truth of what it contained that he sent a full account of all that has been related to Queen Marie Amelia, thus affording her the greatest consolation.

⸰ ELEVENTH DAY ⸰

A Day of Prayer for All the Faithful Who Died during the Past Year

T HE sufferings of Purgatory differ only in point of duration from those of Hell. "Eye has not seen, nor ear heard, nor has the mind of man been able to conceive, the pains that are suffered there." If God rewards as God, He also punishes as God. There are many now suffering in Purgatory who last year during the Month of the Holy Souls [November] advocated the cause of their departed brethren, and who little thought they should so soon pass from this life.

It is not saying too much to call devotion to the Holy Souls a kind of center in which all Catholic devotions meet, and which satisfies more than any other single devotion our duties in that way; because it is a devotion all of love, and of disinterested love. If we cast an eye over the chief Catholic devotions, we shall see the truth of this. Take the devotion of St. Ignatius to the glory of God. This, if we may dare to use such an expression of Him, was the special and favorite devotion of Jesus. Now, Purgatory is simply a field white for the harvest of God's glory. Not a prayer can be said for the Holy Souls but God is at once glorified, both by the faith and the charity of the mere prayer. Not an alleviation, however trifling, can befall any one of the souls but He is forthwith glorified by the honor of His Son's Precious Blood, and the approach of the soul to bliss. Not a soul is delivered from its trial but God is immensely glorified. Moreover, God's glory—His sweetest glory, the glory of His love—is sooner or later infallible in Purgatory, because there is no sin there, nor possibility of sin. It is only a question of time. All that is gained is real gain.

Again, what devotion is justly more dear to Christians than the devotion to the Sacred Humanity of Jesus? It is rather a family of various and beautiful devotions than a devotion by itself. Yet see how they are all, as it were, fulfilled, affectionately fulfilled, in devotion to the Holy Souls. The quicker the souls are liberated from Purgatory, the more is the bountiful harvest of His Blessed Passion multiplied and accelerated. Can the Sacred Humanity be honored more than by the adorable Sacrifice of the Mass? But here is our chief action upon Purgatory. Faith in His Sacraments as used for the dead is a pleasing homage to Jesus; and the same may be said of faith in indulgences, and privileged altars, and the like.

Devotion to our dearest Mother is equally comprehended in this devotion to the Holy Souls, whether we look at her as the Mother of Jesus, and so sharing the honors of His Sacred Humanity, or as Mother of Mercy, and so specially honored by works of mercy; or, lastly, whether we regard her as in a particular sense the Queen of Purgatory, and so having all manner of dear interests to be promoted in the welfare and deliverance of those suffering souls.

Neither is devotion to the Saints without its interests in this devotion for the dead. It fills them with the delights of charity, as it swells their numbers and beautifies their ranks and orders. Numberless patron Saints are personally interested in multitudes of souls. The affectionate relation between their clients and themselves not only subsists, but a deeper tenderness has entered into it because of the fearful suffering, and a livelier interest because of the accomplished victory.

Devotion to the Holy Angels is also satisfied in devotion to the Holy Souls. For it keeps filling the vacant thrones in the angelic choirs, those unsightly gaps which the fall of Lucifer and one-third of the heavenly host occasioned. It multiplies the companions of the blessed spirits. They may be supposed, also, to look with an especial interest on that part of the Church which lies in Purgatory, because it is already crowned with their own dear gift and ornament of final perseverance, and yet it has not entered at once into its inheritance as they did. Many of them also have a tender personal interest in Purgatory. Thousands have clients there who were specially devoted to them in life. Thousands are guardians to those souls, and their office is not over yet.

There is a peculiarity about this devotion for the dead. It does not rest in words and feelings, nor does it merely lead to action indirectly and at the last. It is action in itself, and thus it is a substantial devotion. It speaks, and a deed is done; it loves, and a pain is lessened; it sacrifices, and a soul is delivered. Nothing can be more solid. The royal devotion of the Church is the works of mercy; and see how they are all satisfied in this devotion for the dead. It feeds the hungry souls with Jesus, the Bread of Angels. It gives them to drink in their incomparable thirst His Precious Blood. It clothes the naked with a robe of glory. It visits the sick with mighty powers to heal, and at the least consoles them by the visit. It frees the captives with a heavenly and eternal freedom from a bondage dreader far than death. It takes in the strangers—and Heaven is the hospice into which it receives them. It buries the dead in the Bosom of Jesus in everlasting rest. When the last doom shall come, and our dearest Lord shall ask those seven questions of His judicial process, those interrogatories of the works of mercy, how happy will that man be, and it may be the poorest beggar amongst us, who never gave an alms because he has had to live on alms himself, who shall hear his own defense sweetly and eloquently taken up by crowds of blessed souls, to whom he has done all these things while they waited in their prison house of hope!   —FATHER FABER

Cantipratanus writes of a sick man who was so impatient at the length and severity of his illness that he earnestly begged of God either to restore him to health, or to take him out of the world. God sent an Angel to say to him that he might choose whether he would suffer the pains of Purgatory for three days, or those of his sickness for another year. The sick man thought to himself that the three days would soon be over, while a year of illness meant a long trial of one's patience. He therefore chose the three days in Purgatory. According to his wish, he died and went to Purgatory, but was hardly an hour there when he imagined the three days and even more had expired. He grew exceedingly anxious, sighed, suffered, and wept. "Ah!" he said, "I must be more than a month here, and yet the door is not opened to let me out! I am afraid that he who gave me that choice was not an Angel in reality, but one disguised as an angel, who has shamefully deceived me." While busied with these thoughts, the Angel came to comfort him, and to congratulate him on having accomplished the third part of his atonement. "What!" exclaimed the suffering soul, "the third part! No more than that?" "No more. You have been here but one day; your body is not yet buried." "Ah, holy Guardian Angel!" cried the poor soul, "help me to return to my body and my former sufferings; I would rather endure them patiently for ten years than bear these pains for two days more."

O my God, how we deceive ourselves when we think little of venial sins, and make nothing of them, almost! When we do not penance for our mortal sins—when we blindly look on them as altogether remitted, and forget all about the terrors of Purgatory!

I tremble when I read in the lives of the Saints how severely even the holiest and most faithful servants of God had to suffer for the smallest sins and imperfections. In the *Chronicles of the Friars Minor* we read of one of their number who died at Paris, and who on account of his angelic purity and holiness was looked on as more Angel than man. In the same convent there was at the time a very learned theologian, who was also most enlightened in spiritual matters. He deliberately omitted to say Mass for his deceased brother because he thought it unnecessary to help one who, as he certainly believed, was already high in glory, so great was the fame for sanctity that the deceased had gained during life. But in a few days' time the latter appeared to him, and said in a mournful voice: "Dear brother, for God's sake, have pity on me!" The other, terrified, exclaimed: "Holy soul, what do you want from me?" "Masses! Masses!" was the eager answer, "that I may be released from my torments." "What! You in torments? You who have led such an angelic, innocent, and penitential life! Was not that sufficient purification and atonement for you?" "Alas!" sighed the soul, "no one believes how strictly God judges, and how severely He punishes!" No one believes it! Oh, my dear brethren, how many are there now in Purgatory who are thought to be in Heaven!

St. Antoninus relates in his *Summa* (Part IV, c. x.) that a preacher of his Order appeared a month after his death to the infirmarian of the convent in which he had lived, and told him that he had been kept in Purgatory all that time for no other reason than that he had been too familiar and jocose in his conversations with seculars. A whole month he had to suffer because he had not observed that gravity of demeanor that becomes the religious when in the society of seculars. And how many Masses and prayers had not been offered for him by his brethren in the meantime!

∽ TWELFTH DAY ∽

A Day of Prayer for Deceased Priests and Religious

AS "the Lord found iniquity even in His Angels," many of the priests of the Most High and the spouses of the Lamb may be detained in Purgatory. Let us this day fervently pray for their release: first, because being specially consecrated to His service, He will receive more glory from them in Heaven; and, secondly, because of the succors we derived from them in order to our salvation while on earth.

THE HEROIC ACT OF CHARITY

The Heroic Act of Charity is an offering, a voluntary gift, of all the personal works of satisfaction we may perform during our lives, and of all the suffrages we may receive after our death, to be applied to the relief of the souls in Purgatory. We place all in the hands of the ever-blessed Virgin, praying her to dispose of them as it may please her in favor of the faithful departed. Though this offering has been approved by several Popes, and enriched by many indulgences, some objections have been made to it, which we propose to consider briefly in the following paragraphs.

When devout souls are exhorted to this practice some are wont to reply: "We acknowledge that it would be a great charity to the souls in Purgatory, and therefore very agreeable to God, but it is a complete surrender of that which we ought to cherish most—our prayers and good works. After disposing of all to the Holy Souls, what will remain to discharge our own debts? What can we expect at the hour of judgment if we appear before God stripped of all the merits of our Christian life, and with hands entirely empty? And then to think that we shall no longer be able to direct our prayers as we may desire, either for ourselves or others—for our spiritual or temporal welfare, for our living relatives, friends, and benefactors! Ah, we cannot make such a sacrifice!"

The apparent force of these objections is based upon a false notion of the Heroic Act. A simple explanation of the teaching of theology on this point will be sufficient to assure us that we shall lose nothing, but in reality gain much by this holy practice.

All the acts of our soul when in a state of grace—prayers and good works of every kind—bear a fourfold fruit: of merit, of propitiation, of impetration, of expiation, or satis-faction. Therefore the faithful may, in virtue of a single good work, ask and obtain a favor, appease the anger of God, merit an augmentation of grace here below with a new degree of glory in Heaven, and satisfy the Divine justice. These four qualities, which theology teaches us are proper to each act when one is in a state of grace, are so many mys-terious forces and supernatural powers placed at our dis-posal by the Divine mercy to combat our spiritual enemies and to accomplish our destiny.

Now, what does the Heroic Act require? That we should despoil ourselves of all the merit of our good works? Not at all. It calls for only the fourth part of our good works in favor of the Holy Souls—that is, the expiatory or satisfac-tory part. It is this portion that we place in the hands of Our Blessed Lady to relieve their sufferings or to deliver them from their torments. The meritorious, the propitiatory, the impetratory portion of our spiritual acts remains in our pos-session, belongs personally to us—in fact, cannot be applied by way of suffrage.

Moreover, the cession that we make for the benefit of the Holy Souls augments in value the fourfold qualities of our actions, since their merit is derived from the charity that inspires them; and how can charity be more fully shown than by voluntarily, and through purely supernatural motives, renouncing in favor of our neighbor a spiritual good which belongs to ourselves? Furthermore, we thereby increase our resources a hundredfold; for do we not enlist in our behalf all the souls we thus console or release? And who can express the ardor of their gratitude to their deliverers, the promotion of whose welfare has thus become a sacred obligation to them? This multitude of grateful souls, then, will unite their prayers with ours, and God will refuse them nothing.

The Heroic Act has some analogy to the miracle wrought in the desert, whereby Christ fed five thousand men with five barley loaves and two fishes—that is, He returns to him who had furnished the bread much more than he had originally given. By the charity of this boy the five barley loaves, multiplying under the Divine benediction, not only fed the famishing thousands "as much as they would," but so abundantly that what remained filled twelve baskets. Thus it is with the gifts we make to the Holy Souls; in our hands they are only as five barley loaves, but with the Divine benediction they acquire an extraordinary merit, and not only benefit thousands of suffering souls, but enrich ourselves a hundredfold.

Two points only in the teachings of theology upon Purgatory are illuminated by the infallible rays of Catholic dogma—viz., the existence of a place of detention, and the fact that the prayers of the living are beneficial to the souls therein. All else is veiled in the greater or lesser obscurity of theological opinions. We cannot know what souls are most in need of our prayers, or whether those for whom we pray are in Purgatory or not. No one can tell in what proportion, or according to what law in the Divine economy, our suffrages are available for those for whom we pray. God, indeed respects our intentions, and applies our suffrages in accordance with our desires, when there is in them nothing contrary to His Will. But if the souls for whom we pray are not in Purgatory, our suffrages would fall into the common treasure of the Church, increasing the sum of satisfactory merits, which are applied by way of indulgence to the souls of men. For God cannot, so to speak, traverse the actual order established by His providence, and apply our suffrages Himself directly without in some way receiving from us a sort of authorization to do so—so true is it that the suffering souls can be assisted solely by suffrages. God disposes directly neither of our satisfactory merits, nor of those which compose the treasure of the Church; He passes them over to us; He liberates the souls whom we liberate; He leaves bound those whom we do not unbind—the Poor Souls whom we forget.

It is clear from what has been said above that our suffrages may possibly fail of the object for which we offer them; this can never be the case after we have made the

Heroic Act—our expiatory merits then being placed at the
disposal of the Blessed Virgin, who applies them herself
according to the will of her Divine Son, and who knows all
the secrets of that dread place of purification, which are as
yet concealed from us. We are left entirely free to pray for
any good whatsoever—for our friends, our relatives, our
benefactors, living and dead—and the good God will not fail
to hear our prayers according to our intentions, so long as
they are conformed to His holy Will. Those, then, that make
the Heroic Act of Charity need have but one anxiety—to
multiply the suffrages which they entrust to Our Blessed
Mother.   *—Ave Maria*

Help, Lord, the souls which Thou hast made,
    The souls to Thee so dear,
In prison for the debt unpaid
    Of sin committed here.
These holy souls, they suffer on,
    Resigned in heart and will,
Until Thy high behest is done,
    And justice has its fill.
For daily falls, for pardoned crime,
    They joy to undergo
The shadow of Thy Cross sublime,
    The remnant of Thy woe.
Oh! by their patience of delay,
    Their hope amid their pain,
Their sacred zeal to burn away
    Disfigurement and stain;
Oh! by their fire of love, not less
    In keenness than the flame;
Oh! by their very helplessness,
    Oh! by Thy own great Name:
Help, Lord, the souls which Thou hast made,
    The souls to Thee so dear,
In prison for the debt unpaid
    Of sin committed here.
                              —Cardinal Newman

St. Gertrude having made a donation of all her satisfactory works to the souls in Purgatory, the demon appeared to her a short time before her death, and mocked her, saying: "How vain thou art, and how cruel thou hast been to thyself! For what greater pride can there be than to wish to pay the debts of others without paying one's own? Now, now we shall see the result; when thou art dead thou wilt pay for thyself in the fires of Purgatory, and I will laugh at thy folly whilst thou weepest for thy pride." Then she beheld her Divine Spouse approaching, Who consoled her with these words: "In order that you may know how agreeable your charity for the souls of the departed has been to Me, I remit to you now all the pains of Purgatory which you might have suffered; and as I have promised to return you a hundred for one, I will further increase your celestial glory abundantly, giving you a special recompense for the charity which you have exercised toward My beloved souls in Purgatory by renouncing in their favor your works of satisfaction."

∽ THIRTEENTH DAY ∾

A Day of Prayer for Those Who While On Earth Were Most Fervent in Praying for the Souls in Purgatory

I F we have true zeal for the relief of the suffering members of Christ, we ought to feel a particular interest for such among them as were most fervent in the same cause while on earth. Let us this day use our influence in their behalf.

To the truly fervent Catholic the Church's calendar is

ever replete with the most beautiful symbolism. He who
unconsciously classifies the successive seasons of the year
in accordance with the ecclesiastical rather than the civil
division; he who habitually thinks of Advent and Lent
instead of winter and spring, and in whose vocabulary May,
June, and October are not more familiar terms than are the
months of Mary, of the Sacred Heart, and of the Holy
Rosary—such a one discovers in the physical characteristics
of each season much that harmonizes wonderfully with the
special devotion which Holy Church has associated there-
with.

And if ever such symbolism becomes strikingly manifest,
it is assuredly during the present month, when the age-
stricken year is being hurried to its dissolution. A spirit of
sadness and gloom invests the leafless trees, the bare brown
fields, and sodden meadows; ashen clouds sweep across the
unlovely firmament, and the desolate soughing of the
November winds is incessantly wailing the sad plaint of
each suffering soul in Purgatory: *"Miseremini mei, miseremini mei, saltem vos amici mei."* ["Have pity on me, have
pity on me, at least you my friends." (*Job* 19:21)]. The
depressing aspect of the physical world during this dreary
month must typify to every sympathetic child of the Church
the cheerless and wretched condition of hosts of our
brethren detained in sad and lonely exile from the heavenly
home they long to enter, doomed to wear out a tedious pro-
bation of keenest pain and keenest sense of loss before they
may hope to stand "before the throne . . . clothed with white
robes, and palms in their hands" (*Apoc.* 7:9).

Foremost among the means by which our charity may
best be manifested to the members of the Church suffering
is, unquestionably, our having the Holy Sacrifice offered for
their intention. No other good work, prayer, or mortification
that we can proffer as satisfaction for the uncancelled debts
of the Holy Souls can, of course, be considered as at all com-
parable to this supreme act of infinite worship, meritorious
beyond all else performed on earth. Yet how few, comparatively, are the Catholics who avail themselves of this means

of acquitting themselves of a bounden duty to the faithful departed!

If unable to procure the celebration of as many Masses as we would wish to be offered primarily for the repose of our dead, most of us can apply to them our share in the merits of the daily Mass at which, with very slight inconvenience, we may be present. Next to the charity of having the august Sacrifice celebrated for the specific purpose of aiding some of the Holy Souls ranks this transferring to them of the graces of satisfaction and impetration accruing to all who join with the priest in the offering of the "clean oblation." Never until we ourselves inhabit that land of shadows where our loved ones languish shall we fully appreciate the stupendous effects of a single Mass devoutly attended on behalf of the souls in Purgatory. Happy for us, then, if memory does not reproach us with the careless neglect of hundreds upon hundreds of such charitable acts!

Among other suffrages that certainly alleviate the woes of the Holy Souls is the offering of devout Confessions and Holy Communions. There can be no doubt that earnest petitions addressed to the Eucharistic Christ present in our hearts must be efficacious in procuring relief for those in whose behalf we plead for mercy. If it be a "holy and wholesome thought to pray for the dead" at all times, it cannot but be especially wholesome and peculiarly effective to pray for them at the moment when Jesus, reposing in our bosom, is most willing to accede to our unselfish desires.

Another means of acquitting ourselves of the debt which we owe to these uncrowned saints of Purgatory is to enlist in their cause the potent interest of Our Blessed Lady. Mary is Queen of All Saints, crowned and uncrowned; she is peculiarly the sovereign of the Holy Souls, since among her most distinctive titles are Mother of Mercy, Comfortress of the Afflicted, and Gate of Heaven. She is indeed Queen of Purgatory; and while we may not doubt that, even unsolicited by us, she assists all the inmates of that fiery prison, it is equally certain that those for whom we fervently beseech her powerful intercession will most abundantly reap the benefit of her aid. And so the special devotion of October, the Holy Rosary, should be continued by us throughout the decades of November. Our devout recitation of the beads for the eternal repose of departed relatives or friends will ensure for them the special compassion of the Queen of Heaven, and for us the reward of truest charity.

It is needless to add that the recitation of a number of indulgenced prayers, the giving of alms, the performance of good works of every description, and the accomplishment of acts of mortification of whatever kind, are each and all most excellent methods by which to come to the relief of the vast multitudes whose doleful plaints and piteous supplications call for our sympathy throughout this Month of the Dead. Practically, God has placed in our hands the keys of their prison doors, and, in a sense, it depends upon us whether their blessed ransom shall be effected soon or late. Powerless to help themselves, incapable of meriting either liberation from their bonds or alleviation of their misery, these poor sufferers can but appeal to the friends whom they have left behind on earth, begging earnestly the charity of our assistance.

If ever we entertained for some of those hapless Prisoners of the King sentiments of tender affection, of engrossing love; if ever we rejoiced in their presence and experienced the bliss of their unfailing sympathy; if ever we vowed undying remembrance of their manifold kindnesses, and proffered them the tribute of our enduring gratitude—now is the time to make our protestations, now the time to prove the genuineness of our love.

—REV. A. B. O'NEILL, C.S.C., in the *Ave Maria*

Philip Weld was the youngest son of James Weld, Esq., of Archer's Lodge, Southampton, and a nephew of the late Cardinal Weld. In 1842 he was sent by his father to St. Edmund's College, near Ware, in Hertfordshire, for his education. He was a good, amiable boy, and much beloved by his masters and fellow students. It chanced that April 16,

1846, was a holiday at the college. On the morning of that day Philip had been to Holy Communion at the early Mass (having just finished a retreat), and in the afternoon he went boating on the River Ware, accompanied by one of the masters and some of his companions. Boating was one of the sports which he always enjoyed particularly.

After amusing themselves for some hours, the master remarked that it was time to return to the college, but Philip begged to have one row more. The master consented, and they rowed out to the accustomed turning point. On arriving there, and on turning the boat, Philip accidentally fell into the river, and, notwithstanding every effort to save him, he was drowned.

The corpse was brought back to the college, and the Very Rev. Dr. Cox (the President), as well as all the others, was terribly shocked and grieved to hear of the accident. He was very fond of Philip, and to be obliged to communicate the sad news to the boy's parents was a most painful duty. He could scarcely make up his mind whether to write by post or to send a messenger. At last he resolved to go himself to Southampton.

Dr. Cox set off on the same afternoon, passed through London, and reached Southampton the next day. Thence he drove to Archer's Lodge, the residence of the Weld family; but before entering the grounds he saw Mr. Weld, at a short distance from his gate, walking toward the town.

Dr. Cox immediately stopped the carriage, alighted, and was about to address Mr. Weld, when the latter prevented him by saying: "You need not speak one word, for I know that Philip is dead. Yesterday afternoon I was walking with my daughter Katharine, and we suddenly saw him. He was standing in the path on the opposite side of the turnpike road between two persons, one of whom was a youth dressed in a black robe. My daughter was the first to perceive them, and exclaimed: 'Oh, Papa! Did you ever see anyone so like Philip as that?' 'Like him!' I answered, 'why, it is he!' Strange to say, she thought nothing of the circumstance than that we had beheld an extraordinary likeness of her brother. We walked toward these three figures. Philip was looking with a smiling, happy countenance at the young man in a black robe, who was not so tall as he. Suddenly they all vanished. I saw nothing but a countryman, whom I had before seen *through* the three figures, which gave me the impression that they were spirits. I said nothing, however, to anyone, as I was fearful of alarming Mrs. Weld. I looked out anxiously for the post this morning. To my delight no letter came. I forgot that letters from Ware came in the afternoon, and my fears were quieted, and I thought no more of the extraordinary circumstance until I saw you in the carriage outside my gate. Then everything returned to my mind, and I could not doubt but you came to tell me of the death of my dear boy."

The reader will easily imagine how inexpressibly astonished Dr. Cox was at this recital. He asked Mr. Weld if he had ever before seen the young man in the black robe. The gentleman replied that he had never before seen him, but that his countenance was so indelibly impressed on his memory that he was certain he should recognize him at once anywhere.

Dr. Cox then related to the afflicted father the circumstances of his son's death, which occurred at the very hour in which he appeared to his father and sister; and they felt much consolation on account of the placid smile Mr. Weld had remarked on the countenance of Philip, as it seemed to indicate that he had died in the grace of God, and was consequently happy. Mr. Weld went to the funeral, and on leaving the church after the sad ceremony he looked round to see if any of the ecclesiastics at all resembled the young man he had seen with Philip, but he could not trace the slightest likeness in any of them.

About four months later he and his family paid a visit to his brother in Lancashire. One day he walked with his daughter Katharine to the neighboring village of Chipping, and after attending a service at the church called to see the priest. A few moments elapsed before the Rev. Father was at leisure to come to them, and while waiting they amused themselves by examining the prints hanging on the walls of the room. Suddenly Mr. Weld stopped before a picture which had no name that one could see written under it, as the frame covered the lower part, and exclaimed: "That is the person whom I saw with Philip! I do not know whose likeness this print is, but I am *certain* that he is the one I saw with Philip!" The priest entered the room a moment later, and was immediately questioned by Mr. Weld concerning the print. He replied that it was a picture of St. Stanislaus Kostka, and supposed to be a very good likeness of the young Saint. Mr. Weld was much moved at hearing this, for St. Stanislaus was a member of the Society of Jesus, and Mr. Weld's father having been a great benefactor to the Order, his family was supposed to be under the particular protection of the Jesuit Saints. Also, Philip had been led by various circumstances to a particular devotion to this Saint. Moreover, St. Stanislaus is supposed to be the special advocate of the drowned, as is mentioned in his Life.

The Rev. Father Bateman at once presented the picture to Mr. Weld, who received it with the greatest veneration, and kept it until his death. His wife valued it equally, and at her death it passed to the daughter who saw the apparition at the same time as her father, and it is now in her possession.

The account of this apparition given in a work published in 1875 by the Rev. Frederick George Lee, D.C.L., and in "Glimpses of the Supernatural," is more brief and somewhat inaccurate. The present version, for the most part, is an exact transcript of the testimony of Miss Katharine W. Weld, one of the witnesses of the apparition, the Rev. Father Drummond, S.J., kindly supplying further information.

—Ave Maria

⤳ FOURTEENTH DAY ⤳

A Day of Prayer for the Souls in Purgatory Who during Life Were Most Devoted to the Holy Angels

THE Holy Angels look with special interest on the souls in Purgatory. Numbers of them are guardians to these souls, and long for the moment when they will be permitted to conduct them to Heaven. Many have clients there who fervently invoked them during life. Whole choirs are interested about others, either because they are finally to be aggregated to that choir, or because in lifetime they had a special devotion to it. Again, St. Michael, as Prince of Purgatory and Our Lady's regent, in fulfilment of the dear office attributed to him by the Church in the Mass for the Dead, takes as homage to himself all charity to the Holy Souls; and if it be true that a zealous heart is always a proof of a grateful one, that magnificent spirit will recompense us one day in his own princely style, and perhaps within the limits of that special jurisdiction.

Memory brings back to our minds those who have left us. Through it their features seem present to us; our abodes are filled with their presence. We talk of their actions, their virtues appear attractive, their last words resound in our ears as the legacy of their hearts, as a pledge of their love. Everything reminds us of them—what they said, what they did. Be assured, then, that remembrance is no slight comfort. It renews, no doubt, our grief at their loss, for here below there is no joy without pain—often one gives birth to the other—nevertheless, remembrance is not without its charms. How consoling it is to think of those dearly loved ones. Providence has willed that memory should, in some way, fill up the place of those whom we have lost, and that death, which separates us from all and spares nothing, should at least yield to this power, which impresses on our heart the image of those we mourn.

But of itself is this remembrance, however deep and strong, of any use? None whatever. In vain does it pierce our heart as a sharp arrow, or sink into our minds as a shaft which we carry away with us wherever we go. Does it avail those whom we mourn? No. Is there any means of rendering this remembrance efficacious and fruitful, and of communicating to it a sovereign power? Assuredly there is: *prayer*—prayer, which is a remembrance animated by grace and transformed by faith. This your heart can offer to your parents, your relatives, your friends—all those whom you mourn. "Remember me before God" was St. Monica's last request to her son. The same did your father or your mother, your wife or your sister, on their deathbed address to you. "Remember me." These words imply a remembrance before God as the only thing of benefit to them. On the wings of prayer it flies from the soul as a fiery dart and mounts straight up to the throne of mercy, where God receives it graciously, and sends it back to the poor captive as a message of peace and pardon. Oh, you who seek in the memory of your parents and friends a relief for the suffering their absence causes, give, then, to your sorrow the merit and efficacy that it requires! Remember the departed before God in prayer.

If our merciful Creator, to mitigate the horror of the tomb, has endowed man with the gift of memory, He has, at the same time, placed side by side with it another feeling to console and strengthen us—namely, hope. Memory and hope still remain even when death has deprived us of those we love. What takes deep root in our souls? What survives and soars above all the pangs of affliction? *Hope.* Tossed about by the storms of life, man sees around him only the image of what he has lost, and, amidst the dangers that encircle him, finds in hope his sole consolation. Were this to fail him, his misfortune would be boundless, his pain without relief. God did not allow death, while separating us from our relations and friends, to deprive us of those two things which alone can diminish our regrets—remembrance and hope.

What hopes do we entertain for those dearly loved ones whose remembrance lives in us? That they may have unalloyed happiness; that nothing may keep them from it; that they may have eternal rest. Are not these thoughts sufficient to console and help us when death snatches them from our arms? "May they rest in peace!" are the words which rise to our lips in the days of mourning. "May God receive them, wipe away their tears, satiate them with His love! They have but passed from a life full of misery and pain to one of happiness." *Hope*—such is the supreme and last consolation which remains to us; therefore God in His infinite goodness never draws aside the veil of uncertainty which envelopes the destiny of those we mourn, so that in our grief we may never despair of their future happiness. Whatever may have been the life of those who have preceded us in this valley of tears, however great or numerous their faults, we may always hope they are saved. Our hearts, indeed, feel the necessity of this firm hope. God, according to the words of Holy Scripture, in treating man with respect, did not wish this beautiful feeling to die out of his soul. Perhaps among our dear departed ones there are some who have kept away from their religion, or whom a sudden death has struck down—in youth or in the decline of age—it matters not: hope still lingers, still cherishes a kindly feeling that, in spite of all their faults and sins, Divine mercy has forgiven and the Cross of Jesus Christ saved them.

But if God, together with the comfort of memory, leaves us that of hope, what springs from this hope? what nourishes it? what sustains and strengthens it? Again I repeat—*prayer*. For if prayer is remembrance before God, it is equally Divine hope. If prayer communicates to the remembrance which we preserve of our loved ones its efficacy and fruitfulness, it also gives the confidence of seeing them happy. When we have wept, and sent up to Heaven the Blood of Jesus Christ, that Precious Blood which redeems and purifies; when we have bestowed on those Poor Souls the fruit of our good works, the abundance of our alms, the merits of our penances—then shall we be allowed to hope that God will shorten their sufferings, will break the bonds of their captivity, and admit them to the abode of His glory. Then will a sweet confidence fill our thoughts, and the joys of hope overflow in our hearts. What a comfort to be able to say: "This Communion which I am going to offer for my deceased relations, this sacrifice, this act of virtue which I will perform, this temptation which I will overcome, will perhaps obtain for those I have loved so much an eternal rest, a happiness without end!"

Look with confidence on the Cross of Jesus Christ, behold the wounds of that adorable Saviour, and remember that from them grace and pardon spring forth. From the height of His throne of mercy He extends His arms to draw to His Heart those for whom you weep. He is only waiting for you to ask Him—will you refuse this to those whom you have loved so much? Prayer is, therefore, the only consolation which remains to us; the only offering we can make to those souls who perhaps have loved us too much. But what power does not prayer possess—the prayer often repeated without growing weary? It obtains all, triumps over all, because it draws from the merits of a God-Man an irresistible strength and a sovereign grace.

Pray, then, to Him who with one word can deliver these suffering souls. Listen to their cries from their place of torment: "Oh, you whom we cherished during life, remember us before God! Remember those years passed happily together, when we lived side by side, shared your joys and sorrows, often declared our love for one another—will you forget us now that you no longer see us, now that we suffer and are unhappy? Ah, now is the time to prove your affection by a fervent prayer! God will bless your charity, and will, in return for what you do for us, bestow upon you many graces and blessings. Surely you will not refuse our request! While interceding for us, you will work for yourselves. For a day will come when your neighbors and friends, weeping over your tomb, will say to God: 'Lord, give unto him eternal rest, and let perpetual light shine upon him. *Requiem aeternam dona ei, Domine, et lux perpetua luceat ei!'* Then the Lord will remember your charity toward the dead, will grant the prayer of your friends, and give to your soul refreshment, light, and peace."

St. Bridget had once a vision of Purgatory, and there beheld the souls of the just being cleansed from every stain of sin, as iron is purified in a fiery furnace. She tells us that she heard an Angel calling down the blessing of God upon the charitable Christians who hasten to the rescue of the Poor Souls, for unless they are released by the good works of the faithful, God in His ineffable justice is resolved to purify them by the flames of Purgatory. When the Angel had spoken, there arose a most piteous moan from a great multitude of souls. They entreated the Eternal Judge to forget their many sins, to apply to them the merits of His Sacred Passion, and to admit them into His presence. They besought Him most earnestly to inspire the faithful, but particularly priests and nuns, to offer up prayers, Masses, alms, and indulgences in their behalf, because by doing this they would lessen and shorten their torments, and enable them to enjoy the sooner the beatific vision of Jesus, their love. Suddenly a mysterious light, the brilliancy of which was tempered by a certain dull hue, broke forth and hovered over the dark prison. It was the symbol of approaching deliverance, and the Poor Souls greeted it with acclamations of joy. But they did not forget their benefactors; on the contrary, they asked our Blessed Redeemer to reward a hundredfold the charity of those who had prayed for them.

∾ FIFTEENTH DAY ∾

A Day of Prayer for the Soul
Who Is Richest in Merit

I F YOU can procure by suffrages the release of this soul, you insure to yourself an advocate with God so much the more powerful as this advocate is richer in grace and merit.

––––––––––

What a source of consolation it should be for us that we belong to a Church whose solicitude for all her children extends far beyond the limits of the present life—a Church that, after closing our eyes in this world, will continue her interest for us in the life to come, and never interrupt her supplications until assured that we are in the enjoyment of eternal happiness! How sad and cold must be the belief that can see nothing beyond the grave—which thinks that all is over when the lifeless body has been consigned to the tomb! How worthy of pity are those who thus weep without hope, and who, in receiving the last sight of an expiring friend, think that they are bidding him an eternal farewell!

But for us, who know that death is but the passage to another and a better world, who expect that we shall meet again in eternity those from whom we have been separated in time, how consoling it is to feel that the love of which we were never weary of giving them proofs here below may be shown much more efficaciously now, and that, too, not by costly tributes of affection—not by erecting lofty monuments, which flatter the vanity of the living rather than contribute to the relief of the dead—but by praying for them, by offering to Heaven in their behalf the pleasing sacrifice of our good works.

Among Christian virtues St. Paul tells us that charity is the greatest, and charity is exercised in its highest degree when we aid the poor sufferers in Purgatory, many of whom, perhaps, are suffering there for sins we caused them to commit. It is undoubtedly a great charity to relieve those suffering from corporal necessities, to feed the hungry, to clothe those exposed to cold and nakedness, and to visit the sick cast helpless on their bed of pain. But the object of these Christian ministrations is the body, while that at which we aim by our pious suffrages for the departed is the soul; and insomuch as the soul is above the body, so far also does charity toward the souls in Purgatory exceed in merit that which we bestow on the living. When we relieve the misery of the neighbor we are most frequently moved thereto by natural feelings of pity and compassion. The sight of a fellow being in distress strikes the senses and touches the heart, so that we cannot, as it were, refuse to help him. In relieving the souls in Purgatory, on the contrary, nothing appeals directly to the senses; the soul is purified from all mere earthly motives and emotions, and our charity toward them becomes altogether spiritual. Its merit is proportionately higher, and this should move us to the exercise of charity in their regard with so much the greater zeal.

If God by a special revelation were to make known to any one of us that an immortal soul is indebted to him for the hastening of its hour of eternal bliss, with what faith would he not invoke the protection of this new Saint of Heaven, with what confidence would he not recommend himself to his intercession! This consolation is within the reach of each and every one of us; for though we may not know those whose exile we have shortened, yet we may feel confident that they, seeing all things in God, both know and are mindful of their deliverers. No necessity of addressing them as Joseph of old addressed the servant of Pharaoh, "Remember me when it shall be well with thee," because a soul admitted to the enjoyment of eternal happiness is incapable of being unfaithful to any obligation.

We read in the life of St. Monica that, feeling her last hour at hand, she sent for St. Augustine, and thus addressed him: "My son, I know that I shall soon be no more; but when I am gone pray for the repose of my soul! Do not forget me who have loved you so dearly. Especially think of me when you are at the altar and about to offer the Holy Sacrifice." St. Augustine, bathed in tears, made the required promise, and after his mother's edifying death he never ceased to intercede for her. "God of Mercy!" he exclaimed in his sorrow, "forgive my mother the faults which she may have committed; enter not into judgment with her; turn aside Thy eyes from her sins. Remember that on the point of expiring she thought not of the honors which should be paid to her lifeless corpse; she asked only that she should not be forgotten at Thy altar, in order that any stains of sin which might not have been expiated during her life should be washed away."

Supplications like these, we may confidently expect, will be offered up for us also, if we have secured for ourselves intercessors at the last solemn hour. In like manner will our souls, too, be refreshed by the salutary dew of prayer; and if for the souls of our brethren we have imposed any privations or sacrifices upon ourselves, they will be repaid with interest; for if to give to the poor is to lend to the Lord, what is it to give relief to the souls of our brethren suffering under the avenging stroke of God's justice?

St. Gertrude, whose feast the Church celebrates today, had great zeal in praying for the suffering souls. On one occasion while Mass was being offered for a person of her acquaintance who had died a short time before, the Saint recited five *Paters* in honor of Our Lord's Five Wounds for the repose of her soul; and, moved by Divine inspiration, she offered all her good works for the increase of the beatitude of this person. When she had made this offering she immediately beheld the soul in Heaven in the place destined for her, and the throne prepared for her was elevated as far above the place where she had been as the highest throne of the Seraphim is above that of the lowest Angel. The Saint then asked Our Lord how this soul had been worthy to obtain such advantage from her prayers, and He replied: "She has merited this grace in three ways: First, because she always had a sincere will and perfect desire of serving Me in religion, if it had been possible; secondly, because she had a special regard for all religious and all good people; thirdly, because she was always ready to honor Me by performing any service she could for them." He added: "You may judge by the sublime rank to which she is elevated how agreeable these practices are to Me."

A certain religious died who had always been accustomed to pray very fervently for the Poor Souls in Purgatory, but she had failed in the perfection of obedience, preferring her own will to that of her Superior in her fasts and vigils. After her death she appeared to St. Gertrude adorned with rich ornaments, but so weighed down by a heavy burden which she was obliged to carry that she could not approach to God, though many persons were endeavoring to lead her to Him. As St. Gertrude marvelled at this vision, she was taught that the persons who endeavored to conduct the soul to God were souls whom she had released by her prayers; but this heavy burden indicated the faults she had committed against obedience. Then Our Lord said: "Behold how those grateful souls endeavor to free her from the requirements of My justice and show these ornaments; nevertheless, she must suffer for her faults of disobedience and self-will." The Saint saw that although the soul suffered much, she was consoled and assisted by those whom she had released and by the prayers of the faithful.

After this Our Lord showed St. Gertrude the path by which souls ascend to Heaven. It resembled a straight plank, a little inclined, so that those who ascended did so with difficulty. They were assisted and supported by hands on either side, which indicated the prayers offered for them. Those who were assisted by the Angels had a great advantage, as these blessed spirits repelled the dragons who flew round, endeavoring to prevent their progress. The religious who had lived under obedience were assisted by a kind of railing, placed at each side of this plank, so that they were both supported and protected from falling. In some places these railings were removed, as a punishment to those superiors who had failed to govern their subjects by the rules of obedience. But all the souls who had been truly obedient were assisted and supported by the Angels, who removed every impediment from their path.

A person who had rendered great services to St. Gertrude's monastery being in his agony, the Saint, being engrossed in some pressing occupation, omitted to pray for him. On hearing of his death, she reproached herself for her neglect of one who had always been kind to her Community, and earnestly besought Our Lord to reward him abundantly according to the multitude of His mercies. Our Lord vouchsafed to reply to her: "I have rewarded him for his services in three ways, in answer to the prayers of the congregation. From his natural benevolence, he took the greatest pleasure in conferring favors on others, and I have renewed in him all this pleasure for each act of kindness that he performed. I have also accumulated in his soul all the joy and gratification which he obtained for others by these acts of benevolence, such as giving a child a toy, a poor person a penny [i.e., a small coin], a sick person some fruit, or any other relief; and, lastly, I have made him rejoice exceedingly on account of the approbation which I have manifested for these actions; and I will soon supply all that he needs to attain perfect felicity." —*Life of St. Gertrude*

✍ SIXTEENTH DAY ✍

A Day of Humility to Atone for Souls Suffering for Sins of Pride

THE heart of man is so vitiated that notwithstanding the many motives we have to humble ourselves, we are easily filled with pride. This vice is the first that enslaves us, and the last we subdue. Those who have overcome other bad habits are often ruled by it. Many are suffering for this sin in Purgatory. Let us pray for them today.

An efficacious means of aiding the suffering souls, and one descending to us from Apostolic times, is by the application of indulgences, by which the temporal punishment due to sin is remitted. The merits of Jesus Christ, of His holy Mother and the Saints thus constitute a precious treasury, and as these merits of Our Lord are of infinite value, indulgences may be dispensed from it without limit, but their dispensation is reserved to the pastors of the Church, and especially to the Sovereign Pontiff. There are indulgences for the living—that is to say, those which one may gain only for oneself—and there are others which the living are enabled to apply to the relief of the souls departed. How merciful does not Our Lord show Himself in thus multiplying means of helping the suffering souls!

Indulgences are either *partial*, which remit only a portion of the temporal punishment due to sin, or *plenary*, by which, when gained, the entire debt of temporal punishment is forgiven. Consequently, if a partial indulgence be obtained for the souls in Purgatory, it ordinarily satisfies for a portion of their debt to God's justice; while if a plenary indulgence be applied for them, it is sufficient to atone for all their demerits, to obtain their immediate release from their prison of agony, and admission to the endless joys of Paradise. Oh, how much good each one of us may do for Purgatory! We all have there a legitimate mission; we can do everything provided only that we are inclined, and the more generously the Church places her treasures at our disposal in favor of the suffering souls, the more inexcusable shall we be if we do not take advantage of them.

To gain indulgences two things are indispensable—that we be in the state of grace, and that we duly perform the prescribed duties. It is well to remark that persons who are accustomed to confess their sins every week may gain as many indulgences as occur within the week without a new confession, also that one Communion suffices for gaining several plenary indulgences for the faithful departed; but for each indulgence, prayers should be recited for the intentions of the Church [that is, of the Holy Father].

A Precious Indulgence Applicable to the Souls in Purgatory

In the catalogue of indulgences published by Pius IX there is one which many perhaps have failed to notice. It is as follows: "An indulgence of 100 years and 100 quarantines [periods of 40 days] may be gained once a day by the members of the Confraternity of the Rosary, provided that, contrite for their sins, they carry the beads about them in honor of the ever-blessed Virgin" (ix., n. 3).*

Much as we may, with reason, value the indulgence of 500 days for each grain which the Sovereign Pontiffs have authorized the Crosier Canons to attach, yet while reciting the beads, or the chaplet, thus indulgenced, we gain very little more than one-half the indulgences granted by Pius IX in favor of those who simply carry the Rosary about their persons.

We may remark:

1. There can be no doubt of the authenticity of this indulgence, as it is attested by the catalogue published in 1862 by order of the Sovereign Pontiff.

2. One hundred years and 100 quarantines make a total of over 40,000 days' indulgence.

3. To gain this indulgence it is necessary to be a member of the Confraternity of the Rosary. It will not suffice to belong to the Perpetual Rosary, or to the Living Rosary.

4. It is not necessary that the beads should be worn

---

* All the partial indulgences mentioned in this chapter would seem, unfortunately, to have been revoked and superseded by the new *Enchiridion on Indulgences* which was issued by the Sacred Apostolic Penitentiary on June 29, 1968 in obedience to the Apostolic Constitution "The Doctrine of Indulgences" issued by Pope Paul VI on January 1, 1967. In these documents, partial indulgences are no longer specified as representing days, years or quarantines. See Appendix 2 herein for information on the current regulations on "How to Gain a Plenary Indulgence." —*Publisher,* 2005.

exteriorly, after the manner of Religious. It is sufficient that they be carried about one's person—in one's pocket, for example—in order to gain each day upward of 40,000 days' indulgence.

5. It is not required that the whole Rosary of fifteen decades should be thus carried; the ordinary five-decade beads will suffice.

6. It is unnecessary that it should be worn at night. It is, however, a very pious and laudable custom to have the beads always at least near at hand.

7. Besides this, there are a great many other indulgences attached by Pius IX to the recitation of the beads. A few among them are: 7 years, 7 quarantines; 100 days for each *Pater* and *Ave*; 50 years when the beads are said in a church of the Confraternity, or, where this is not possible, in any other church or oratory.

Be careful, then, always to carry your beads. It is a practice which will furnish an occasion of gaining precious indulgences for the souls in Purgatory and for your own benefit. It will also be a constant expression of your love for Mary. The child who loves his mother is always happy to carry about him an object which she in her love has given him.   —*Ave Maria*

———

Those who wear the Blue Scapular can, by reciting 6 *Paters*, 6 *Aves*, and 6 *Glorias* in honor of the Blessed Trinity, of the Immaculate Conception, and for the intentions of the Church, gain *each time* all the indulgences of the Seven Basilicas of Rome, of Portiuncula, of St. James of Compostella, and of the Holy Land; 20 years for each visit to the sick; 60 years for half an hour's daily meditation.

———

St. Mary Magdalen de Pazzi had assisted in her last moments a member of her Community who died with the reputation of great sanctity. The sisterhood not only lost no time in reciting for her the usual Offices, but also applied in her behalf all the indulgences which it was in their power to gain. The body was laid in the church exposed to view, and St. Mary Magdalen from the grating gazed upon it with feelings of tenderness and devotion, while she offered fervent prayers for the eternal repose of the sister. Suddenly she saw the soul of the deceased, beaming with light, arise from the cold remains and ascend to Heaven, there to receive the crown of eternal glory. The Saint, at the sight, could not refrain from exclaiming: "Farewell, Sister, farewell, happy soul, who enterest Heaven before thy body has been committed to the tomb. What a happiness! What glory! In the bosom of the Eternal Spouse be not forgetful of us poor mortals who still pine and sigh on earth." Then Jesus Himself appeared to console her, and told her that this soul had been thus promptly delivered from Purgatory and admitted to Heaven by virtue of holy indulgences. Thenceforth the zeal of the sisters for gaining indulgences was such that each one would feel a scruple unless she tried to obtain every one she could. Let us imitate the piety of these good religious, and if we but possess the requisite dispositions, we cannot fail to deliver many souls from Purgatory.

Sacred Heart of Jesus, have mercy on us.
(100 days' Indulgence)
Immaculate Heart of Mary, pray for us.
(100 days' Indulgence)
Our Lady of the Sacred Heart, pray for us.
(100 days' Indulgence)
Sweet Heart of Jesus! be Thou my love.
(300 days' Indulgence)
Sweet Heart of Mary! be my salvation.
(300 days' Indulgence)
May the Sacred Heart of Jesus be everywhere loved.
(100 days' Indulgence)
Jesus, meek and humble of heart, make my heart like unto Thine.
(300 days' Indulgence)

My Jesus, mercy!
(100 days' Indulgence)
My sweetest Jesus, be not to me a Judge, but a Saviour.
(50 days' Indulgence)
Eternal rest give unto them, O Lord, and let perpetual
light shine upon them.
(50 days' Indulgence)

TO OUR BLESSED LADY FOR THE SOULS
IN PURGATORY

O turn to Jesus, Mother! turn,
   And call Him by His tenderest names;
Pray for the Holy Souls that burn
   This hour amid the cleansing flames.

Ah! they have fought a gallant fight,
   In death's cold arms they persevered;
And after life's uncheery night,
   The harbor of their rest is neared.

In pains beyond all earthly pains,
   Favorites of Jesus, there they lie,
Letting the fire wear out their stains,
   And worshipping God's purity.

Spouses of Christ they are, for He
   Was wedded to them by His Blood,
And Angels o'er their destiny
   In wondering adoration brood.

They are the children of thy tears;
   Then hasten, Mother! to their aid;
In pity think each hour appears
   And age while glory is delayed.

See how they bound amid their fires,
   While pain and love their spirits fill;
Then with self-crucified desires
   Utter sweet murmurs, and lie still.

Ah me! the love of Jesus yearns
　　O'er that abyss of sacred pain,
And as He looks His bosom burns,
　　With Calvary's dear thirst again.

O Mary! let thy Son no more
　　His lingering Spouses thus expect;
God's children to their God restore,
　　And to the Spirit His elect.

Pray, then, as thou hast ever pray'd;
　　Angels and Souls all look to thee;
God waits thy prayers, for He hath made,
　　Those prayers His law of charity.
　　　　　　　　　　　—FATHER FABER

∽ SEVENTEENTH DAY ∾

A Day of Prayer for Souls Suffering for Sins of Anger and Impatience

"**L**EARN of Me to be meek," says Our Blessed Lord. But few frequent His school, few relish His doctrine. Many, otherwise well-disposed, injure their own souls and cause unhappiness to others by their little attention to, or practice of, this Divine lesson, and, dying without having done penance, are consigned to the flames of Purgatory. Offer today for their relief some acts of mortification.

———————

At the time when Our Blessed Lord walked upon the earth there was in Jerusalem a certain pool where the sick and those afflicted with bodily diseases were wont to congregate. At certain times an Angel of the Lord came down and stirred the waters, and the sick man who went first into the pool after the visit of the Angel was healed of his infirmity. When Jesus came there He found a man so infirm that he could not, in the least degree, assist himself, and he had been waiting day after day for eight-and-thirty years, while others who were stronger than he, or who had friends to help them, went down before him and were healed. Our Lord asked him why he had not availed himself of the blessing which God at times had given to the waters, and he answered in words that are full of deepest and most mournful pathos: "Lord, I have no man who, when the water has been stirred, will cast me into the pool."

In those few words what a story is compressed of the tedious passing of weary years! He had come there a youth, with hope in his heart that he would soon be cured of his infirmity, and many a long year seemed to spread before him in which he might enjoy his recovered health. But the years passed by, and those who were boys along with him grew to be men, and many a change had passed upon the faces that he knew; many a sunrise did he see in hope, and many an evening closed in the disappointment of the hope deferred that maketh the heart sick; and his hopes were dying out, and his hair was growing grey, when, after nearly forty years, Jesus came and cured him.

What a sorrowful story! Eight-and-thirty years of waiting—the certain remedy before his eyes, and *none* to help him to avail himself of its efficacy! Friends he may have had—one friend he surely had, when his mother held him in her arms. But his mother was dead, and time and the chance and change of life had dispersed his early friends; or, after the manner of the world, in the day of his distress they had forsaken him. In that weary march of lonely years what want of human feeling that man had witnessed! What cool contempt, what silent carelessness! And we are tempted to exclaim against a city whose annals are disgraced by a story such as this. But pause before one bitter thought forms itself in your mind, before one word of condemnation rushes to your indignant lips. Stay a little.

There is a certain place in the Church of God—a place

which you have not seen with the eye of flesh, but which faith teaches you exists as really as the places you have walked in and that you know with the familiar knowledge of everyday experience. It is a land over which hangs a cloud of silent sorrow, of uncomplaining agony that is voiceless in the intensity of its resignation. And in that silent land of pain lies many a friend of yours whom your heart cannot forget—friends whom you knew once, whose faces, whose smiles, whose voices, were familiar to you in days gone by; who were members, it may be, of the same household; who knelt with you at the same altar; who worked and prayed and smiled, and were bound to you by every tie which the kindly charities of nature and of grace can forge. They died, and they are in Purgatory. Stricken are they by no mere earthly malady, but by an agony for which earth has no image nor any name. Consumed are they by no mere earthly fever, but by the fever of a fire that searches their very soul. And you pass by—you, their friend—and you have at your disposal the healing flood of the Precious Blood of Jesus! You pass by—heedless or forgetful or indifferent, it matters little which: you pass by and give no help! You leave the sufferers there, looking up with pain-stricken, wistful eyes to the Heaven above, and saying, "O God, we have no friend who, when the healing Blood of Thy Divine Son is ready in the Holy Mass to extinguish the flames of our torment, will use it for our relief!" Condemn if you will, in what sharp terms indignation may suggest, the heartlessness of the citizens of Jerusalem, but do not omit to compare it with your own, when, either through carelessness or forgetfulness, you neglect to do your part—the part of friendship, the part of charity—to assist the suffering souls in Purgatory.

—*Sermons of the Rev. Joseph Farrell*

How real death, and that which will come after death, ought to be to us, since we have not only been told of death, but have seen death's hand on those who stood by our side! Good and true as these were, we do not imagine that they

were undefiled enough to enter at once into the presence of
the living God. We cover their graves with garlands; we
never speak of them without a sigh; we say life is not the
same to us—but when November comes we do not give
them special thought or prayer! And yet we know as certainly as we know anything that it is our prayers they
crave.

> "Pray for my soul. More things are wrought by prayer
> Than this world dreams of. Wherefore, let thy voice
> Rise like a fountain for me night and day.
> For what are men better than sheep or goats
> That nourish a blind life within the brain,
> If, knowing God, they lift not hands of prayer,
> Both for themselves and those who call them friend?
> For so the whole round earth is every way
> Bound by gold chains about the feet of God."

Last year we grudged nothing to the friend that has since
left us; and if any sacrifice could bring him back, we say fervently that we would make it. Last year we would have
traveled miles to be near him were he ill. We should have
spurned the thought that any mere inconvenience could
keep us from him were our presence needed. Had he not
grappled us to him with a thousand hooks of steel during a
thousand days? A father, a brother, a friend—it matters not
which—it may be that we have lost all. How, now that the
time has come for showing our gratitude, do we keep our
promise?

Who dares to say that to give this dear soul solace, to
repay it for the love it had for us, to keep the pledges we
made to it, we would not cross the sea a hundred times? And
yet when it comes to the mere matter of crossing a few
streets, of rising a little earlier in the morning, of having
some Masses said, we hesitate, we procrastinate, we forget!

There are the mocking *immortelles* of last year, scarcely
changed in color, hung on the railings around his grave;
there is the memorial, on the carved letters of which no
moss has had time to grow; there are all the remembrances

of the dead mutely speaking to us at every turn. They cry out to us of the great fact, but we do not hear—we have "ears, and hear not." In that future, which shall come as surely as next November, shall we, in our purgation, be heard?   —MAURICE FRANCIS EGAN, in the *Ave Maria*

The following is an extract from the Life of Saint Margaret Mary:

Mother Philibert Emanuel de Montoni, Superioress of the Convent at Annecy, whose memory is held in veneration, and whose holy life is a subject of edification for the entire Institute, died February 5th, 1683, in the time of Mother Greffier's superiority, and was by her particularly recommended to the prayers of Saint Margaret Mary. After some time she told her superior that Our Lord had shown her that this soul was very dear to Him because of her love and fidelity in His service, and that He had prepared an ample reward for her in Heaven after her purification in Purgatory was ended. Finally, He showed her this soul receiving great relief in her sufferings by the application of the suffrages and good works which were offered for her throughout the whole Order of the Visitation. Saint Margaret praying again for this holy superior on the night of Holy Thursday, Our Lord caused her to see her being placed, as it were, under the chalice which contained the Sacred Host, there receiving a share in the merits of His Agony in the Garden of Olives. On Easter Day, which that year fell on the 18th of April, she saw her approaching beatitude, desiring and hoping soon to enjoy the sight and the possession of God. At length, on Sunday, the 2nd of May, the Feast of the Good Shepherd, she saw her in eternal glory, chanting melodiously the canticle of Divine Love.

Thus we see that this holy and fervent superioress, animated with the purest spirit of her Institute, having died on the 5th of February with the reputation of sanctity, only entered into the enjoyment of glory on the 1st of May, as was revealed to Saint Margaret Mary: God, in order to purify her, deferring her happiness for eighty-six days. So long a Purgatory for so fervent a soul is a lesson for those who always think they do too much for the service of God, and who applaud themselves for the lightest practices of penance. What time and what suffering will not be necessary to expiate their faults in Purgatory!

∽ EIGHTEENTH DAY ∾

A Day of Prayer for Souls Suffering for Sins of Intemperance

MANY, very many, it is to be feared, are suffering in Purgatory on account of habits of intemperance in which they indulged during life. Offer in atonement for them today to the Eternal Father the thirst His Divine Son was pleased to suffer on the Cross.

––––––––––

When intense pains are of long duration there is nothing more intolerable. Such is the case in Purgatory. Some persons appearing a few hours after their death declared that they imagined themselves confined within its burning precincts entire years. Indeed, it is of this place of torments we may say that one day there is equal to a thousand elsewhere. A single quarter of an hour in this place of woe is frightful in the extreme. If a person were condemned to be burned alive he would deserve our compassion, though his torments would soon end. These are terrifying truths; but, alas! we are little or not at all affected by them. Thus we every day hear it said at the death of some person: "It is well for him to be delivered from his sufferings; his pains are now at an end; he is happy in being released from them"— not reflecting on the violent torments he is suffering in Purgatory, if God has had so much mercy on him. Oh, how great is the blindness of men!

Let us do all we can to alleviate the sufferings of those who are undergoing their purification. With such measure as we mete to others, it shall be measured to us again. We shall find compassion in the other life in proportion as we shall have acted mercifully in this. God, in the designs of His all-holy will, has marked out a certain economy from which He does not ordinarily depart. Consequently, though the suffrages of religion are not wanting to any of the faithful departed, yet by a just dispensation of Divine Providence it may happen that they bring but comparatively slight relief to those who have shown themselves insensible with regard to Purgatory; while, on the contrary, they who shall have manifested a merciful and charitable disposition in this respect shall experience through the Divine favor the effects of an abundant compassion. Let us merit this favor for ourselves at present, that we may not wish for it when it will be too late hereafter.

Two distinguished members of the Dominican Order, Father Bertrand and Father Benedict, were one day engaged in the discussion of the question—whether it is an act of greater charity to labor for the relief of the souls in Purgatory or for the conversion of sinners? Father Bertrand took the latter view, and said that Our Divine Lord came on earth expressly to seek and save the sinner—that he is in continual danger of being eternally lost, and that to co-operate in his salvation is to participate in the work of redemption; while, on the other hand, he argued that the souls in Purgatory are already in a state of security as to their future felicity, and that if they suffer torments it is only for a time, after which they shall enjoy the endless glories of Paradise.

Father Benedict defended the cause of the Holy Souls in Purgatory, and remarked that Our Blessed Lord after His death descended in person to deliver them; that if sinners are immersed in sin the fault is their own; that they can, with God's grace, free themselves whenever they so wish;

while the souls in Purgatory are detained in cruel sufferings without the possibility of doing anything toward their
own relief. That in the same way as it would be more praise-
worthy to assist a poor invalid who has not the use of his
limbs than a mendicant who is strong and need not remain
in wretchedness except from choice, thus also is it more
meritorious to concern oneself about the souls in Purgatory
than about sinners, though, of course, well-regulated charity will be solicitous about both.

But Father Bertrand did not yield to these strong arguments, and in consequence Our Lord permitted one of the
suffering souls to come to him at night bearing a heavy burden, which he placed on the shoulders of the religious, caus-
ing him almost intolerable fatigue and pain. He thus
understood by experience the truth which he had argued
against in his discussion. From that time forth he applied
himself with great diligence to the aid of the Suffering
Souls, and became as remarkable for devotion to them as
before he had appeared wanting in that respect. It would
appear as if the authority of St. Thomas might be quoted on
the side of Father Benedict, as he says: "Prayer for the dead
is more acceptable than for the living, for the dead are in
greater need of it, and cannot help themselves as the living
can."

Marie Denise de Martignat, of the Visitation Order, was
never weary of praying for the Suffering Souls. She was
continually accompanied by them, and their presence was
sensible to her. She told her superioress that so far from
being afraid, she was as much at her ease amid a troop of
these souls as when with her sisters in community, and that
she found more profit for her soul in conversation with
them than with the living. Her superioress once expressed
a wish to be visited by a soul from Purgatory, if the visit
would make her more humble and more acceptable to God.
Marie Denise replied: "Certainly, my dear Mother. If such is
your courage and your desire, let us pray Our Lord to grant

it you." The superioress having consented, she was astonished that same evening at receiving a mysterious sign from a Suffering Soul, who from that moment became her frequent visitor. At the end of several months Marie Denise told the superioress that the continuance in the pains of Purgatory of such a soul as the one who had visited her would teach her how much longer souls are detained in that suffering than she had supposed before.

The Feast of Our Lady of Angels was a day on which Marie Denise generally obtained the liberation of many souls from Purgatory. Once, after Holy Communion on that day, she felt a strong interior movement as if Our Lord was taking her soul out of her body, and leading her to the shore of Purgatory. There He pointed out to her the soul of a powerful prince who had been killed in a duel, but to whom God had given the grace to make an act of contrition before he breathed his last; and she was ordered to pray for him especially. She was so overcome by the vision of this soul that the superioress perceived that something extraordinary had happened to her. She related the vision, and added: "Yes, my dear Mother! I have seen that soul in Purgatory; but, alas! who shall deliver it? Perhaps it will not come out till the Day of Judgment. Oh, Mother!" she continued, weeping, "how good is God in His justice! How has this prince followed the spirit of the world and the flesh! How little anxiety has he had for his soul, and how little devotion in the use of the Sacraments!"

The effect of this vision, and of her penances for this soul, had such an effect on her bodily health that the superioress remonstrated with her on the subject; but she replied that she must now suffer incessantly, as she had offered herself to God in order to procure some alleviation of pain for that Poor Soul. "And yet, my dear Mother," she said, "I am not so much moved at the lamentable state of suffering in which I have seen his soul as I am struck with wonder at the blessed moment of grace which accomplished his salvation. That happy instant seems to me an outflow of the infinity of God's goodness, mercy and love. The action in which he

died deserved Hell. It was no attention to God on his own
part which won from Heaven that precious moment of
grace. It was an effect of the Communion of Saints, by the
participation which he had in the prayers that were offered
for him. The Divine Omnipotence lovingly allowed itself to
be turned by some good soul, and in that, grace acted
beyond its wont. Ah, my dear Mother! Henceforth we must
teach everyone to beg of God, Our Blessed Lady and the
Saints, that final instant of grace and mercy for the hour of
death, and also to pave the way for it by good works;
because, though Our Lord may sometimes derogate from
His ordinary Providence, we must never presume on that
privilege in our own case. Many souls have been lost in the
very action in which the Prince was saved. He had but one
instant of life in the free possession of his mind in order to
co-operate with the precious moment of grace; that moment
inspired him with a real contrition, which enabled him to
make an act of true, final repentance. As he had not lost the
Faith, he was like a match ready to take fire; so that when
the spark of merciful grace touched the Christian center of
his soul, the fire of charity was kindled and brought forth a
saving act. God made use of the instinct which we naturally
have to invoke our First Cause when we are in urgent peril
of losing the life which we hold from Him; and thus He
touched the Prince, and drew him to have recourse to efficacious grace. Divine grace is more active than we can even
conceive. We cannot wink our eyes as quickly as God can do
His work in the soul where He seeks co-operation; and the
moment in which the soul makes its act of co-operation with
grace is almost as brief as the one in which it receives it;
and in this the soul experiences how admirably it has been
created in the image and likeness of God."

Language almost fails to describe the sufferings, both of
mind and body, which Marie Denise went through for the
alleviation of this soul. Mother de Chaugy devotes a whole
chapter to them, and they are quite equal to those which are
read of any of the Saints. After a long martyrdom of this
kind, it pleased God that she should see in a vision the suf-

fering soul of the Prince, slightly raised above the bottom of the burning abyss, and in a capacity of being delivered somewhat before the Day of Judgment, and also that an abbreviation of *some few hours* of his Purgatory had been granted. She begged Mother de Châtel to pray for him; and that good mother consenting to do so, could not refrain from expressing her surprise that Marie Denise had only spoken of an abridgment of a few hours; but the sister replied: "It is a great thing that the Divine Mercy has begun to allow itself to be influenced; time has not the same measure in the other life which it has in this; years of sadness, weariness, poverty and severe illnesses in this world are not to be compared with one single hour of the sufferings of the Poor Souls in Purgatory."

It would take too long to relate all the communications Our Lord vouchsafed to make to her about the state of that soul. It came at last to this—that she offered her life for his simple alleviation, not deliverance, and it was accepted. Not long before her death, when the superioress was expressing herself to the effect that surely by this time the soul was free, Marie Denise said with great warmth: "Oh, Mother! many years and many suffrages are needed yet." And at last she died, and yet there was no word that the Prince was delivered, even by that heroic sacrifice, crowning upwards of nine years of suffering, prayers, Masses, Communions, and indulgences not on her part only, but through her on the part of many others also. What a long commentary might be written upon all this! But hearts that love God will comment on it for themselves. Blessed be His most glorious Majesty for its insatiable purity!   —FATHER FABER

⌒ NINETEENTH DAY ⌒

A Day of Charity to Atone for Souls Suffering for Sins against This Virtue

IT is to a want of charity that we are to attribute those rancors and petty dislikes that are so common in the world. Where are they who sincerely pardon their enemies and love those who have injured them? Even on their deathbed they find it difficult to forgive. Yet without charity there is no admission to Heaven—the abode of charity. Let us pray fervently today for those who are suffering for sins against this holy virtue, and let us try carefully to avoid all failings of this nature, that we may not have to expiate them in the flames of Purgatory.

There are, as we all know, two worlds—the world of sense and the world of spirit. We live in the world of sense, surrounded by the world of spirit, and as Christians we have hourly and very real communications with that world. Now, it is a mere fragment of the Church which is the world of sense. In these days the Church Triumphant in Heaven, collecting its fresh multitudes in every age, and constantly beautifying itself with new Saints, must necessarily far exceed the limits of the Church Militant, which does not embrace even a majority of the inhabitants of earth. Nor is it unlikely, but most likely, that the Church Suffering in Purgatory must far exceed the Church Militant in extent, as it surpasses it in beauty. Toward those countless hosts who are lost we have no duties; they have fallen away from us; we hardly know the name of one who is there. We are cut off from them; we have no relations with them.

But by the doctrine of the Communion of Saints, and of the unity of Christ's mystical body, we have most intimate relations both of duty and affection with the Church Triumphant and Suffering; and Catholic devotion furnishes us with many appointed and approved ways of discharging these duties toward them. For instance, God has given us such power over the dead that they seem to depend almost more on earth than on Heaven; and surely, that He has given us this power, and supernatural methods of exercising it, is not the least touching proof that His Blessed Majesty has contrived all things for love. Can we not conceive the joy of the blessed in Heaven, looking down from the bosom of God and the calmness of their eternal repose upon this scene of dimness, disquietude, doubt, and fear, and rejoicing in the plenitude of their charity, in their vast power with the Sacred Heart of Jesus, to obtain grace and blessing day and night for the poor dwellers upon earth? It does not distract them from God; it does not interfere with the Vision, or make it waver and grow misty; it does not trouble their glory or their peace. On the contrary, it is with them as with our Guardian Angels; the affectionate ministries of their charity increase their own accidental glory.

The same joy in its measure may be ours, even upon earth. If we are fully possessed of this Catholic devotion for the Holy Souls we shall never be without the grateful consciousness of the immense powers which Jesus has given us on their behalf. We are never so like Him or so nearly imitate His tender offices as when we are devoutly exercising these powers. We are humbled excessively by becoming the benefactors of those beautiful souls who are so immeasurably our superiors, as Joseph was said to have learned humility by commanding Jesus. While we are helping the Holy Souls we love Jesus with a love beyond words—a love that almost makes us afraid, yet also with a delightful fear, because in this devotion it is His hands we are moving, as we would move the unskillful hands of a child. Dearest Lord, is it not incredible that He should let us do these things?—that He should let us do with His satisfactions what we will, and sprinkle His Precious Blood as if it were so much water from the nearest well?—that we should limit the efficacy of His unbloody Sacrifice, and name souls to Him, and expect Him to obey us, and that He should do so?

Beautiful was the helplessness of His blessed infancy;

beautiful is His helplessness in His most dear Sacrament; beautiful is the helplessness in which for the love of us He mostly wills to be with regard to His dear spouses in Purgatory, whose entrance into glory His Heart is so impatiently awaiting! What thoughts, what feelings, what love should be ours as we, like choirs of terrestrial angels, gaze down on the wide, silent, sinless kingdom of suffering, and then with our own venturous touch wave the sceptred hand of Jesus over its broad regions, all richly dropping with the balsam of His saving Blood!   —FATHER FABER

———————

Among the many instances of pious munificence which the life of Eusebius, Duke of Sardinia, presents, it is recorded that he devoted the revenues of one of his richest cities to the benefit of the suffering souls in Purgatory. But his powerful neighbor, the King of Sicily, panting for military glory, and even more eager for plunder, declared war against him, and appearing unexpectedly before this very city with a formidable army, made himself master of it. This loss was more keenly felt by Eusebius than would have been the loss of half his dukedom. Determined, therefore, on defending his rights, he assembled his troops without delay. Notwithstanding his great inferiority in point of numbers, he boldly marched against the usurper, relying on the hope that the justice of his cause would supply for the inequality. On the day of battle, while both sides were preparing for the attack, it was announced to Eusebius that, besides that of his rival, another army was descried approaching, whose banners and uniform were completely white. This unforeseen event at first disconcerted him, and suspending his preparations, he sent forward two heralds on horseback to demand of the newcomers whether they were friends or enemies. But lo, from the ranks of the unknown army four cavaliers advanced, and announced that they belonged to the heavenly host and were come to recover the city of suffrage! The allies then united and advanced against the common enemy. Losing courage at seeing himself opposed by two armies, and having learned whence the new auxiliaries had come, the King of Sicily at once sued for peace, offering to restore the conquered city, and to make, moreover, twofold compensation for the injury he had done. These terms were accepted. When Eusebius turned to thank his supernatural allies, the chief explained to him that their ranks were exclusively composed of those who had been freed from Purgatory through his means, and that they watched unceasingly over his welfare. The good Duke took occasion from this to become more than ever devoted to the souls in Purgatory, whose powerful protection he experienced to the last.

"REQUIEM ÆTERNAM"

"Eternal rest and endless light,"
　　So prays, O Lord, Thy Church on earth
　　For those who wait the second birth
Within the tomb's apparent night.
And is not this a prayer inspired?
　　In simple words, how much expressed!
　　"Eternal light and endless rest,"
What more remains to be desired?

Rest for the busy hand and brain,
　　Rest for the weary toil-stained feet;
　　For the poor heart that rest complete
Forever sought on earth in vain.
And *Light*—God's primal gift of old—
　　All life's strange problems now explained,
　　All knowledge without toil attained,
All mysteries as a scroll unrolled.

　　　　　　　　　　　　　　—S. M. S.

∽ TWENTIETH DAY ∽

A Day of Prayer for Souls Suffering in Purgatory on Our Account

ST. Paul assures us that charity is the greatest of Christian virtues; and charity is exercised in its highest degree when we aid the poor sufferers in Purgatory, many of whom, perhaps, are suffering there for sins we caused them to commit. Let us pray very earnestly for them today.

In order to form some idea of the sufferings endured by the souls in Purgatory, let us represent them to ourselves as they really are, prisoners to the Divine Justice. Imprisonment, even in this mortal life, when complete, solitary, harsh and long, is a terrible torture. Alone with your thoughts, your love and your sorrow; alone—far from the light, whose rays no longer visit you; far from men, who no longer know you; far from hearts that no longer pity you; there, within four walls, with no companion save solitude, darkness, silence and weariness—suffering, still to suffer, always to suffer—measuring the time by sighs, as the pendulum by its oscillations. Oh, tell me, can you comprehend this torture? Listen to an historical trait, more eloquent than a long discourse.

A man had sighed away many years in a well-known prison. One day, weary of suffering, he conceived a hope of release. There was a woman in those days whose influence was great enough and her hand strong enough to break the prisoner's chains and set him free. Behold, says the historian, in what eloquent terms the unhappy man made his appeal. "Madame, the 25th of this month, 1760, I have suffered one hundred thousand hours, and there still remain two hundred thousand hours for me to suffer." He had counted them all! Yes, as you might count, one by one, the ticking of the clock during the long, weary night when suffering drives sleep away.

If such can be the sufferings of prisoners on earth, what shall we say of prisoners in the invisible world? Who shall tell us of the duration of time they suffer? For we do not measure the duration of time as it passes, but as we feel it pass; and the slowness of its passage increases in proportion to the pains we suffer. For the souls in Purgatory minutes are long days, days are long years, and years are ages that seem unending. A religious after his death appeared to one of his brethren and revealed to him that three days passed in Purgatory seemed to him longer than three thousand years. Another, having in an extraordinary state experienced the torture of Purgatory merely from Matins until dawn, felt persuaded that he had suffered during one hundred and fifty years. Thus these prisoners in Purgatory, far more than earthly prisoners, count the long hours that so slowly pass, and in their sufferings they seem endless.

—FATHER FELIX, S.J.

A certain mother, inconsolable at the death of her only son, wept for his loss long and bitterly, without, however, helping him by those means which religion affords. To give her affection a useful direction, God sent her a vision. She beheld a procession of youths, clad in white garments, enriched with various ornaments, and directing their joyous course towards a magnificent temple. This temple represented Heaven, the white garments were the garb of faith, and the ornaments upon them were the works of charity. The bereaved mother, having her lost son unceasingly in her mind and heart, anxiously sought for him among this chosen band, but her searching glance could not discover him till all the rest had passed. She then beheld him, but clothed in a dark and sullied robe, and she saw that he advanced but slowly and with difficulty. This sad sight caused her tears to flow anew, and, with a voice broken with sobs, she exclaimed: "Why, O my son, are you so sad, and differ so much from your companions? Why do you remain so far behind?" The young man sorrowfully replied:

"Mother, you see these mournful and sullied garments. Behold in them what your obstinate grief and tears for me produce! Your unreasonable grief weighs heavily upon me and impedes my progress. Ah! Cease to abandon yourself to mere natural feelings, and, if you truly love me, if you desire to see me happy, arouse your faith, and aid me by works of faith and charity. Assist me by your pious suffrages, as is done by other mothers not less affectionate, but more wise and more religious than you. Then I shall be enabled to join the happy company you have seen, and attain to that heavenly bliss for which I long with so much ardor." Without saying more he disappeared, leaving his mother as eager to procure him spiritual help as before she had been remarkable for giving herself up to useless grief.

May similar sentiments of faith animate us with regard to our departed friends, and render us more mindful of aiding and consoling them by meritorious works than of abandoning ourselves to unprofitable grief and sadness for their loss.

Saint Margaret Mary, praying one day for two persons of rank in the world who had died, one of them was shown to her as condemned for several years to the pains of Purgatory, notwithstanding the solemn services and the great number of Masses that were offered for her. All these prayers and suffrages were applied by the Divine justice to the souls of some families subject to her who had been ruined by her want of charity and equity in their regard; and as these poor people had left nothing after their death to obtain prayers for their souls, God supplied them in this way. The other person was in Purgatory for as many days as she had lived years upon earth. Our Lord made known to Saint Margaret Mary that amongst all the good works this person had performed He had had particular regard to certain humiliations she had received in the world, which she endured with a truly Christian spirit, not only without complaint, but even without mentioning them, and that in reward He had been mild and favorable in His judgment.

A gentleman, father to one of the novices, being dead, was

recommended to the prayers of the Community at Paray. The charity of Saint Margaret Mary, then Mistress of Novices, induced her to pray more particularly for this person, and on the novice repeating her request for her prayers some days after, she said: "Be satisfied, my child; he is in a state to benefit us by his prayers instead of needing ours." She then added: "Ask your mother what generous action her husband performed before his death, for it is that which made the judgment of God favorable to him." The novice did not see her mother until the time of her Profession. She then asked what this act of Christian generosity was, and learned that when the holy Viaticum was given to her father, a butcher of the town joined those who accompanied the Blessed Sacrament, and placed himself in a corner of the room. The sick man, perceiving him, called him by his name, told him to approach, and, cordially pressing his hand, asked his pardon, with a humility very unusual in persons of high rank, for some severe words he had said to him some time before, and was desirous that everyone should witness the satisfaction he made him. Saint Margaret Mary had learned from God alone what had passed, and the novice knew by this the truth of what had been revealed to her holy Mistress regarding the happy state of her father.

✑ TWENTY-FIRST DAY ✑

A Day of Prayer for Souls Whom Our Blessed Lady Is Most Desirous to Have Released from Purgatory

THIS being the Feast of the Presentation of Our Blessed Mother, the glorious Virgin Mary, in the Temple, let us employ it in procuring the release of souls who were devout to her during life, and whom she is most desirous to present in the Temple of the Living God, that the days of their mourning may be ended.

Truly happy are the devout clients of Mary, our most merciful Mother: for she not only assists them by her prayers in this life, but also relieves and consoles them by her protection in Purgatory. Since these souls are in great need of succor, and unable to assist themselves, she feels a special solicitude to obtain relief for them. St. Bernardine of Sienna says that in that prison where souls are detained Mary has a certain dominion and plenitude of power, not only to relieve them, but even to deliver them from their sufferings.

With regard to the mitigation of their pains, the same Saint, applying to Our Blessed Lady the words of Ecclesiasticus, "In the waves of the sea I have walked," adds, in her name, "I have walked in the waves of the sea, visiting my devout servants, who are my children, relieving their necessities and assuaging their pains." He says that the pains of Purgatory are called waves because they are transitory, unlike the pains of Hell, which never end; and they are called waves of the sea, because they are very severe. Mary frequently visits and relieves her clients who are afflicted with these torments. Behold, then, says Novarino, the great advantage of being a servant of this good Lady; she cannot forget her servants when they are afflicted with the pains of Purgatory, and, although she relieves all these suffering souls, she obtains greater indulgence and succor for those who were devoted to her on earth.

Our Blessed Lady said once to St. Bridget: "I am the Mother of all the souls in Purgatory, and the pains which they merit for the sins they had committed during life are, as long as they remain in that place of suffering, hourly mitigated in some measure by my prayers." This merciful Mother even sometimes condescends to enter into that holy prison to visit and console her afflicted children. How great is the consolation she obtains for them in the midst of their torments! St. Bridget heard Our Divine Lord saying one day to His Mother: "Thou art My Mother; thou art the

Mother of Mercy; thou art the consolation of the souls that are in Purgatory." And the Blessed Virgin herself said to the Saint, that as a poor sick person, bedridden, suffering, and abandoned, is refreshed by every word of comfort, so these suffering souls are consoled by the bare mention of her name. The name of Mary—a name of hope and salvation, which these her beloved children frequently invoke in that prison—is to them a source of great consolation. "The loving Mother," says Novarino, "as soon as they invoke her name, prays to God for them and obtains relief, so that the burning heat of their torments is, as it were, cooled by a celestial dew."

But Our Lady not only consoles and relieves her clients in Purgatory, she also delivers them from their sufferings and prison by her intercession. On the day of her glorious Assumption it is said that the prison of Purgatory was emptied. Novarino states that it is related by grave authors that Mary, when she was about to ascend to Heaven, asked of her Son the privilege of bringing with her all the souls that were then in Purgatory. "From that day," says Gerson, "the Blessed Virgin possesses the privilege of delivering her servants from the pains of Purgatory." St. Bernardine of Sienna asserts absolutely that Our Lady can, by her prayers, and by the application even of her own merits, rescue souls from Purgatory, and particularly the souls of those who were devoted to her on earth. Novarino says the same: he thinks that by the merits of Mary the sufferings of these souls are mitigated, and even shortened, because by her intercession she obtains an abridgment of the time of their detention. To obtain their deliverance it is enough that she present herself before her Son, to pray for them through His merits.

St. Peter Damian relates that a certain woman, called Marotia, appeared after death to her godmother, and said that on the Feast of the Assumption Our Blessed Lady delivered her from Purgatory, together with a multitude of souls, which exceeded in number the inhabitants of Rome. Denis the Carthusian writes that on the festivals of

Christmas and Easter, Mary descends into Purgatory, accompanied by legions of Angels, and delivers many souls from their sufferings. And Novarino is inclined to think that the same happens on each of the solemn festivals of Our Blessed Mother.

The promise made by Our Blessed Lady to Pope John XXII is well known. She appeared to him and said that those who wore the [brown] scapular and died in the state of grace would be delivered from Purgatory on the Saturday after their death. This, as Crasset relates, the same pontiff declared in a Bull which was confirmed by Alexander V, Clement VII, Pius V, Gregory XIII, and Paul V; and this latter in a Bull published in 1612 said that "Christians may piously believe that the Blessed Virgin will assist by her continual intercession, by her merits, and special protection after death, and principally on Saturday (which is the day the Church has consecrated to Our Lady), the souls of the members of the Confraternity of Holy Mary of Mount Carmel, who shall have departed this life in the state of grace, shall have worn the scapular, observing chastity according to their state, and shall have recited the [Little] Office of the Virgin, and if they have not been able to recite it, will have observed the fasts of the Church, abstaining from flesh-meat on Wednesday [and Saturday], except on Christmas Day." In the solemn office of the Festival of Holy Mary of Carmel we read that it is piously believed that the Blessed Virgin, with maternal love, consoles the brothers of Mount Carmel in Purgatory, and by her intercession conducts them soon into the Kingdom of Heaven. Why should not we, if we are devoted to this good Mother, expect the same graces and favors?

—St. Alphonsus Liguori, *Glories of Mary*

The following lines, supposed to be written from Heaven, may give some idea of the sentiments of a soul delivered from Purgatory by Our Blessed Lady.

"I had been long in Purgatory. Slowly waved to and fro

the waves of living fire above, beneath, around me. They penetrated my whole being, burning out the stains and remnants of my sins and purifying my whole nature. It was agony! Yet with what deep gratitude is not each pang endured, for the suffering soul knows it is thus brought nearer to Jesus and to Heaven! It was a solemn Feast of Our Blessed Lady. The mighty waves of fire began to ebb away like the flow of a returning tide. Light like no earthly light lit up our gloom and dimmed the fiery flames. Bright Angels passed me in procession; they were the guardian spirits of the souls in Purgatory hastening to present their clients to Mary, Sovereign of this realm of purgation. I felt she would pass by my place of suffering. Would she lessen its duration? As Jesus wills so wills Mary, and the Poor Souls in Purgatory have no will but theirs, so I waited, patient yet hopeful, for the passage of the Queen of Angels and of men. I had seen her on other festivals, and each time she had consoled me. Now, as she passed me, she paused. I cannot describe the wonderful beauty of her countenance. There is a mild, inexplicable grace in Mary; her look is all mercy and gentleness, and her purity is betokened by the robes of shining light she wears. They seem woven of diamonds and pearls and the tears she has wiped away. Her mild eyes were bent on me. She extended her hand, and signed to my Angel Guardian, 'Be that captive free.' In an instant I beheld myself stainless and free from all my bonds: my garment shone as rays of many-colored lights, and I joined the group of happy souls who followed the Mother of Mercy. We passed on in her train through the prison of the Justice of God, and many others shared in the clemency of Mary. Then we left the halls of penance, and passed from the depths of the earth toward the glorious center of the universe, the rest and dwelling of the sacred Humanity of Jesus—the home called Paradise! Far swifter than the light were we borne toward it, and its mighty portals rose at our approach. The land of song, the land of beauty, the dwelling place of light, joy, and happiness appeared before me. Exiles of earth, breathe the choicest odors, listen to the sweetest sounds, rejoice in the deepest affections, view the most enchanting beauty, and in your hearts shall awaken one faint touch of the thrilling sensations of heavenly life!'

In the *Life of St. Teresa [of Avila]* we read the following: "A monk, to whom I owed a great debt of gratitude, and who had formerly occupied the post of Provincial in his Order, was on his deathbed. As soon as I heard of it, I was much afflicted, and felt great uneasiness regarding his soul, although he had always lived a virtuous and edifying life.

"Knowing how onerous is the care of souls and the responsibility it entails, and knowing that my friend had spent twenty years in this ministry, I could not refrain from being anxious on his account. I threw myself, therefore, at Our Lord's feet, and prayed to Him earnestly to deliver that soul from the pains of Purgatory, and in reparation for any errors he might have committed, to accept for him any good I might have done in my life, together with the infinite merits of His Sacred Passion.

"My prayer ended, I seemed to behold that soul rise from the depths of the earth, and with an expression of the most intense joy mount up to Heaven. Although I knew that this priest was already far advanced in years, his face appeared to me as that of a young man under thirty years of age, radiant with youth. The apparition was of short duration, and left me much consoled, and I was no longer anxious about the lot of that soul, as about that of many others whom I have held in equal affection. As he died at some distance from me, it was not till a long time after that I became acquainted with the circumstances of his happy death."

◇ TWENTY-SECOND DAY ◇

A Day of Prayer for the Souls in Purgatory Who Were Most Devoted to the Sacred Heart

OUR Divine Lord loves the poor sufferers in Purgatory with an infinite love and ardently desires to receive them into Heaven. Let us try to gain many indulgences today for those who, while on earth, most loved and honored His Sacred Heart.

The devotion to the Holy Souls is so full of doctrine, and embodies so much that is supernatural, that we need not be surprised at the influence it exercises over the spiritual life. In the first place, it is a hidden work from first to last. We do not see the results, so that there is little food for vainglory; neither is it a devotion, the exercise of which appears in any way before the eyes of others. It implies, moreover, an utter ignoring of self by making away with our own satisfactions and indulgences, and keeping up a tender interest in an object which does not directly concern ourselves. It is not only for the glory of God, but it is for His greater glory, and for His sole glory. It leads us to think purely of souls, which it is very difficult to do in this material world, and to think of them, too, simply as spouses of Jesus. We thus gain a habit of mind which is fatal to the spirit of the world and to the tyranny of human respect, while it goes far to counteract the poison of self-love. The incessant thought of the Holy Souls keeps before us a continual image of suffering, and not of merely passive suffering, but of a joyful conformity to the Will of God under it. Yet this is the very genius of the Gospel, the very atmosphere of holiness.

Furthermore, it communicates to us, as it were by sympathy, the feelings of those Holy Souls, and so increases our trembling yet trustful devotion to the adorable purity of God; and as, except in the case of indulgences applied to the dead, it requires a state of grace to make satisfaction for the sins of others, it is a special act of the lay priesthood of the members of Christ. The spirit of the devotion is one of pensiveness; and this is an antidote to frivolity and hardness, and tells wonderfully upon the affectionate character which belongs to high sanctity. Who can tell what will come after patient years of thus keeping constantly before our eyes a model of eagerness, unspeakable, patient eagerness, to be with our dearest Lord? What a wonderful thing is the life of a fervent Catholic! It is almost omnipotent, almost omnipresent, because it is not so much he who lives as Christ who liveth in him. What is it we are touching and handling every day of our lives, all so full of supernatural vigor, of secret unction, of Divine force?—and yet we consider not, but waste intentions and trifle time away in the midst of this stupendous supernatural system of grace, as unreflecting almost as a stone embedded in the earth and borne round unconsciously in its impetuous revolutions day by day. (FATHER FABER)

Mother Gabriel de Colombière, of the Incarnation, was one of the Ursulines of Poitiers who went to found the Monastery of Loudun. She passed the remainder of her life there in the practice of solid virtue to the great edification of all with whom she lived. Her superiors testified that her obedience was perfect and that she was most faithful in following the movements of Divine grace. For three years before her death she suffered much from asthma, and bore her sufferings with admirable patience, without relaxing in any way her assiduity at the regular observances, and particularly at the Divine Office and Mental Prayer, in which she found all her consolation. She died on the 1st of November, 1660, aged sixty-three, and in her forty-first year of Profession.

She had often said during her life that if God showed her mercy and accepted her desires she would return after her death to declare to Mother Mary of the Angels what she would have known in the light of eternity for the salvation and perfection of the Community. The zeal and desires of this holy Religious were agreeable to God. In the following words Mother Mary relates to Father Surin, S.J., the circumstances of the apparition: "On November 6th, 1660," she writes, "I felt myself strongly urged to ask of God that it would please Him to show mercy to good Mother Gabriel, and if she did not yet enjoy glory to give it to her through the merits of the Precious Blood of Jesus Christ His Son, and through the intercession of the Blessed Virgin whose holy scapular she had worn. What obliged me to make this petition was, that the whole night I had my imagination filled with the thought of this dear mother; and often since her death, although I wished to persuade myself that she enjoyed the happiness of Heaven, my heart was troubled when I thought of her. In fine, I felt myself pressed to ask Our Lord that, if it were for His glory and the good of several others, He would make known to us her state. A short time after, she presented herself to me with a very mild countenance, appearing more humiliated than suffering, although I saw well that she suffered much. At first, seeing her near me, I was very much frightened, but as there was nothing terrifying in her appearance, I was soon reassured I made the Sign of the Cross. I asked Our Lord not to permit me to be deceived on this occasion, and I recommended myself to my holy Guardian Angel. I asked her in what state she was, and if we could render her any service. She replied that she was satisfying the Divine Justice in Purgatory. I begged her to tell me what detained her there, if God wished that she should tell it to me for our instruction. She heaved a deep sigh, and said: 'It is on account of several acts of negligence in the common exercises of regularity, also for a facility in yielding to the bad and imperfect sentiments of others, but still more for the habit of retaining little things and disposing of them according to my wants, or according to my natural inclination. God sees things very differently from the way in which *we* look on them; and if during life souls knew the injury they do to God and to themselves by not applying seriously to their perfection, and how much they will have to suffer to expiate their weaknesses, their human respect and self-indulgence, they would have more facility in overcoming themselves and more firmness in following the lights of grace.' I begged her to tell me how our Community and I could remedy this evil. She replied: 'In general, they fail much in submission of judgment; interior recollection, charity in bearing with their neighbor, and subjection to obedience. I have failed much in these things during my life.' I asked if we could render her any service. She replied: 'I desire ardently to see and possess God, but I am content to satisfy His justice as long as it shall please Him.' I inquired if her suffering was great. 'It is,' she said, 'incomprehensible to those who do not feel it.' She then begged me to pray for her, and disappeared.

"On the night of the 30th of the same month, Mother Gabriel again appeared to me and gave me to understand that she was undergoing a part of her Purgatory among us—that she hoped to go to enjoy God on the Feast of the Immaculate Conception of the Blessed Virgin, and that this amiable Mother and St. Joseph, to whom she had been greatly devoted, had obtained mercy for her; that her Purgatory would have been long but for their aid. She told me that the greater number of religious had much to satisfy the Divine Justice for in the other life, because they had not a proper application to the ordinary actions of religion, which they perform through routine, and that this has no excuse before God. I asked her what the soul suffers. She answered: 'The soul feels within herself an ardent desire which, like a devouring fire, urges her to go to unite herself with her God, and she sees herself bound and kept back by a thousand little nets and cords which are consumed only very slowly by the activity of the fire. Her understanding is enlightened by a light which shows her the means that she had to break these bonds during her life, and the reproaches of her conscience make known to her that she has through self-love turned aside from the way of grace to follow that of nature and the senses, for which she condemns herself. She sees the designs that God had formed regarding her, with the want of correspondence on her part, and this sight is to her a great torment on account of the exceeding goodness that she sees in God, and her own ingratitude.'

"On the 8th of December, 1660, between five and six in the evening, Mother Gabriel appeared to me surrounded by a brilliant light and said: 'The goodness of God permits me to tell you that I go to enjoy Him. Adieu, my dear Mother; labor for eternity to which you aspire, and assure mortals that whatever is not done, said, or suffered for God, serves only for pain and torment. There are many souls deceived in their practices.' I begged her to be our advocate with God. She assured me that she would and that she would pray for us. I recommended to her certain persons who had begged me to do so. She received my request with much goodness and kindness, without saying anything distinctly, and approaching the window which looks on the altar where the Blessed Sacrament reposes, made a profound genuflection. After that, an Angel who was with her took her as if by the hand. Both were raised on high and disappeared from my eyes, leaving my heart full of joy for the glorious state of this happy soul."

❧ TWENTY-THIRD DAY ❧

A Day of Prayer for Those Who Died Suddenly and without Preparation

HOW worthy of compassion is the lot of those who are suddenly called out of life to the dread tribunal of God's Justice, who are summoned to meet the Bridegroom when they least expect it; for, though clothed in the wedding garment of grace, its whiteness may just then be tarnished; though provided with the oil of charity to feed their lamps, it may burn somewhat dimly. Let us pray fervently for such souls today.

Is there anything more painful than to see a beloved friend, brother, and even perhaps a parent, die without the last Sacraments, unprepared and unrepentant? What bitterness, what terrible anguish of mind, what a wound for the poor heart! The dearly-loved one thus lost to us forever! Never, we imagine, shall we see him again; all during eternity no call will ever reach him, no answer will ever come, or, rather, from the terrible abyss moans and cries of despair will be heard. O God! What unutterable suffering! In the light of faith nothing could be more bitter. He whom I so justly loved, whose salvation was as dear to me as my own, death has suddenly seized: he did not frequent the Sacraments, and was not in a state of grace. Behold now all is over forever. Nothing remains but to weep eternally, and it almost seems as if death itself will not be able to make good his loss to me, for how taste of its sweetness, remembering him who suffers eternally, and for whom I would have given my life?

These forebodings are, alas, only too natural! But let us be careful not to exaggerate them. The mercy of God, like His greatness, is an abyss. We do not know, and we have no right to say, that such a person is damned, no matter how he died. His feet, it is true, were in the road to perdition, and he exposed himself to the terrible sentence, this is quite certain; but still the mysteries of the last moment, and especially those of Divine Goodness, are hidden from us. An illustrious bishop once said: "Between the last sight of a dying person and eternity there is an abyss of mercy, especially if some pious persons have been praying for him." God knows what is for the best, and in His own good time may have granted the prayers which we thought unheard. What was wanting to this agonizing person? A ray of light, with the last beatings of the heart, and this instantly produces a feeling of love and sorrow. That suffices! Hell is closed and Purgatory opened. Jesus, casting a glance on the soul about to leave the body, says: "Which dost thou prefer, the demon or Me?" Raising its eyes to Him, the soul answers: "Thee,

Lord, oh, Thee!" and mercy triumphs.

In the Rabbinical book we read those beautiful words attributed to God: "Open the doors of repentance as wide only as the eye of a needle, and I will open the doors of mercy so wide that you could enter on a chariot with four horses." Who knows but that God has allowed you to survive the deceased on purpose to intercede for him? So wonderful and so unfathomable are the designs of Providence! For all eternity we shall adore them. Let us repeat the consoling words of St. Chrysostom, so well calculated to soothe the bitterness of our grief—"Imagine a spark falling into the sea. Can it exist? Can it be seen? Such is your wickedness compared with the goodness and mercy of God. But even this comparison fails to convey an adequate idea of the God-head, for the sea, vast as it is, has limits, whereas the mercy and goodness of God are boundless."

This consideration, however, should not encourage the sinner to put off his conversion and penance under pretence that God will pardon him at the last moment; for does not Our Lord say, "Watch and pray, for death will come like a thief in the night," and that judgment will depend upon the light and grace we have received? But the deceased for whom we are justly alarmed—had he all the spiritual advantages which we enjoy? Will not God take into account his ignorance, the bad example he received, the impetuosity of a passionate nature, want, perhaps, of intelligence and judgment, the corrupt surroundings in which his lot was cast? Who knows but that your future prayers known to God have had some influence on the Divine mercy? And here a word of advice to parents to carefully watch over the Christian education and training of their children may not be out of place. He who has no religion follows, perhaps, with tears the body of a cherished father, mother, or brother to the grave, but when all is over he strives to banish from his mind the sad memory. . . . Never does he offer a prayer, never does he perform a good work for those souls who may, on his account, be now suffering the torments of Purgatory. Think well on this, you fathers and mothers, and do not neglect a duty which so nearly concerns you!

Well, then, let us pray much, let us pray often, let us pray always for our loved departed ones. "Men are more intelligent than wicked, more blind than wicked." At each one's death, at the tribunal of God, the Saviour of men will say: "Father, forgive them, for they know not what they do." Placed under the law of hope, no less than that of faith and love, the thought of the infinite goodness of our Divine Redeemer should encourage us in our trials. Let us, then, never cease to hope and address humble and persevering prayers to the Lord, for we know not where they will be granted. Great Saints and learned Doctors have written most consoling things on the powerful efficacy of prayer for those cherished souls, whatever may have been their end. One day we shall know the ineffable wonders of Divine mercy. We should therefore never fail to implore it with great confidence.   —REV. F. PASTEL

OUR KIND FATHER

There's a wideness in God's mercy,
    Like the wideness of the sea,
There's a kindness in His justice,
    Which is more than liberty.

There is no place where earth's sorrows
    Are more felt than up in Heaven,
There is no place where earth's failings
    Have such kindly judgment given.

For the love of God is broader
    Than the measure of man's mind,
And the Heart of the Eternal
    Is most wonderfully kind.

But we make His love too narrow
    By false limits of our own;
And we magnify His strictness
    With a zeal He will not own.

If our love were but more simple,
We would take Him at His word;
And our lives would be all sunshine
In the sweetness of the Lord.
          —FATHER FABER

An eminent musician named Herman Cohen was converted from the Jewish religion to the light of the True Faith by witnessing a miraculous manifestation of the Sacred Host at the moment of Benediction. Having embraced Christianity, he shortly after abandoned the world and entered the Order of Mount Carmel. Full of grateful devotion toward the Blessed Sacrament, he used to pass daily several hours prostrate before the Tabernacle in adoration, and with great fervor earnestly prayed for the conversion of his mother, whom he ardently loved. Prayers, fasting, good works of every kind for this intention seemed sweet to his soul. Notwithstanding all his efforts, her conversion did not come to pass. She died, to all appearance, in the errors of Judaism. A wonderful grace, however, was vouchsafed her by the Divine Mercy at the last moment of her life, and it was made known to a very holy person that her soul was saved. The account is as follows:

"On the 18th of October, 1860, after Holy Communion, I found myself in one of those moments of intimate union with Our Lord wherein He makes me so sweetly feel His presence in the Sacrament of Sacraments. After a few moments He made me hear His voice, and deigned to give me some explanation regarding a conversation that I had had the day before. I remembered then that in this conversation one of my friends manifested to me her astonishment that Our Lord, who had promised everything to prayer, had, nevertheless, remained deaf to those Father Herman had so often offered to obtain the conversion of his mother. Her surprise had almost reached discontent, and I had considerable trouble to make her understand that we should adore the justice of God and not seek to penetrate His secrets. I ventured to ask my Jesus how it was that He, who is goodness itself, had been able to resist the prayers of Father Herman, and had not granted him the conversion of his mother. This was His answer: 'Why does _____ always try to sound the depth of My judgments and seek to penetrate mysteries she cannot understand? Tell her that I owe My graces to no one, that I bestow them on whom I please, and that in acting thus, I cease not to be Justice itself; but let her also know that rather than fail in the promises I have made to prayer I would overturn heaven and earth, and that every prayer that has for object My glory and the salvation of souls is granted when it possesses the necessary qualities.' He added: 'To prove to thee this truth, I will make known to thee what occurred at the moment of the death of Father Herman's mother.' My Jesus enlightened me then with a ray of His Divine light, and made known to me, or rather, made me see in Him, what I shall endeavor to relate.

"At the moment when Father Herman's mother was on the point of yielding her last breath, she appeared deprived of consciousness and with scarcely any sign of life. She saw our Immaculate Mother present herself to her Divine Son, and prostrate at His feet, heard her say to Him: 'Mercy, pity, O my Son, for this poor soul who is about to be lost for all eternity! Do I entreat of You for the mother of my servant Herman what he has so often asked. The soul of his mother is infinitely dear to him; a thousand times has he consecrated it to me. He has confided it to my tenderness and the solicitude of my heart. Can I suffer it to perish? No, no, this soul is mine; I will have it! I claim it as my inheritance, as the price of Your Blood, and of my sorrow at the foot of the Cross.' Scarcely had the blessed suppliant ceased speaking when a strong, powerful grace issued from the source of every grace, the adorable Heart of Jesus, and triumphing instantaneously over her obstinacy and resistance, that soul turned immediately with loving confidence toward Him whose mercy had preserved her even in the arms of death, and she said to Him: 'O Jesus, God of Christians!

God that my son adores, I believe, I hope in You, have mercy on me!' In this exclamation, heard by God alone, and which issued from the most intimate depths of the heart of the dying one, were included a sincere regret for her obstinacy and her sins, a desire of Baptism, and an express wish to receive it, and to live according to the rules and precepts of our holy religion if she could have returned to this life. This impulsive act of Faith and Hope in Jesus was the last sentiment of this soul, and at the moment she made it ascend toward the throne of the Divine Mercy, the feeble bonds which retained her within her mortal frame broke, and she fell at the feet of Him who had become her Saviour before being her Judge. After having shown me all these things, Our Lord added: 'Make this known to Father Herman; it is a consolation I desire to bestow on him for his long sorrow, that he may bless the goodness of My Mother's heart and its power over Mine.'"

Father Herman's mother died in 1855. The vision or favor was granted in 1860, and in 1861 he received the original of this letter.

✐ TWENTY-FOURTH DAY ✑

A Day of Prayer for Souls Suffering For Sins of Detraction

SILENCE kept in a spirit of devotion brings great solace to the Suffering Souls. There are few who do not sin by the tongue, and Purgatory is filled with souls who suffer for having given that member too much liberty. Offer today for their relief some acts of self-denial.

———————

When a mariner has lost his chart and compass, and finds himself the sport of wind and wave, he is glad to direct his bark across the troubled waters by the faint and flickering gleam of the distant stars; so, too, men who have lost the Faith, and who know nothing of the infallible authority of the Church, are glad to appeal to mere human reason to pilot them over the dangerous and turgid ocean of life.

One who believes a doctrine merely because it is reasonable, because it satisfies his mind, or because it sounds plausible, may be a most excellent Protestant, and may act fully up to the principle of private judgment, but he is no Catholic. The faith of a Catholic rests upon much higher grounds than mere reason. Whatever the Church teaches will of course be reasonable, because it is true, but whereas with a Catholic a doctrine is *reasonable because it is true,* with a Protestant *it is true because it is reasonable*. As an instance in point we may refer to the doctrine of Purgatory. Though it has been scoffed at, and derided, and turned out of doors, and misrepresented and caricatured, we know it to be true, because we have the Church's warrant for it, and the Church is "the pillar and ground of truth." But, on the other hand, if it be true, it must of necessity be reasonable likewise; and the task before us now is to make this fact clear—to show even according to unaided human reason and common-sense that it is a necessary postulate; that, in short, to deny Purgatory is impossible, without doing violence to reason.

If we look out upon the world and examine the lives of different men, we shall find that they fall naturally into three distinct groups. The first is but a small one. It consists of those highly favored souls, few and rare, who spring up perfect creations of Divine grace and power; souls around whom an altogether special Providence seems to keep guard: whom God never seems to let out of His hands, even for an instant; but whom He shields from every danger, and saves from every fall. They are, as it were, the picked fruit, the choice specimens of earth, made, one might almost fancy, for the express purpose of exhibiting the omnipotence of God's protective love and fostering care. Such was St. John the Baptist, sanctified in his mother's womb; and St. John, "the disciple whom Jesus loved," and who laid his

head on his Master's breast; such also was the chaste and
gentle St. Joseph, the foster father of Christ; and such,
above all and before all and beyond all, was the Virgin,
immaculate and all pure, whose very name carries with it
an aroma of sweetness and perfection, inspiring joy and
gladness. Souls upon whom the shadow of sin has never
fallen, who were ever faithful to grace and loyal to God—
these form the first division of the human family. What
becomes of them? Where is their dwelling place and their
home? Ah, with them to die is to go to God! Death is but the
passage from earth to Heaven; but the rending of the veil
that shuts out the glorious vision of eternal peace. All their
lives long they had been nestling on God's breast, and death
to them was only as the gentle shock with which we awaken
a sleeping child—they opened their eyes only to gaze
entranced on the beauteous face of Him they loved.

Then there is another class who form a marked contrast
to these. A class consisting of men without religion and
without love: men who make up what the Scripture calls
the "World" when it says, "The world is the enemy of God."
These are persons who may be honored, esteemed, and
made much of by men. They may dwell in rich houses and
sumptuous palaces, and may have many friends and a wide
acquaintance and considerable influence; they may be much
spoken of, and flattered and sought after, but their souls are
steeped in iniquity. Men who know not God, and do not care
to know Him, but who pass their lives in sin, and spend
their years in forging for themselves chains which eternity
will not wear through, and fetters which will hold them fast
in the dungeons of Hell forever—if they die with mortal sin
on their soul, unrepented and unconfessed.

Were these two the only classes, there would be little difficulty in dispensing with a Purgatory. Just as the first class
of mankind that we have considered rise at once to Heaven,
so this last sinks at once to Hell. There is no difficulty so far.

But, in addition to the absolutely spotless and the mani-
festly reprobate, is there not another and a larger body of
Christians who can be classed under neither of these cate-

gories, who have neither the perfection of the first nor the diabolical wickedness of the last; persons who are neither strikingly virtuous nor strikingly vicious, who do not arrest our attention or make us pause to marvel either at their piety on the one hand, or their depravity on the other; men of ordinary virtue, of decent, regular lives, honest, sober, truthful, modest; men who have their faults and their failings, and who are striving with a greater or less earnestness against them; men who fall, and perhaps occasionally fall grievously, but who struggle up again, and go on their way resolved to do better? What is to become of such as these when they come to die? Suppose death were suddenly to overtake them, into what invisible region would their souls wing their flight? Would they ascend at once, all stained and bespattered with the slime of earthly imperfection into the very bosom of God? Or must we perforce consign them straight away to the land of eternal darkness and to the pool of quenchless fire? Is there no third alternative? According to the popular Protestant teaching there is not.

We will take a typical case. Suppose a man living in the great dreary city of London, or Liverpool, or Manchester—a married man, of mature age. He is a lawyer, or a doctor, or a man of business. He spends the greater part of the day in the exercise of his profession or trade. He enjoys life; he shares its amusements and its recreations; he is respected and trusted, and has many friends. His business will not permit him much time for religious practices, though it must be confessed that he gives less even than he might. He goes to Mass, at least on Sundays, though he studiously avoids the sermon; he says his morning and evening prayers, but he would rather we did not inquire too nicely into the fervor and earnestness that accompanies them; he confesses his sins, but his purposes of amendment are not very firm, and he takes no great trouble to atone for sin by any self-imposed penance.

He has his faults, and he is not altogether unconscious of them; nay, he regrets them, though he may not make any sustained effort to overcome them. Then he is irritable, or quarrelsome, or harsh to his subordinates, or he is too unmeasured and unrestrained with his tongue. He falls into many imperfections, he commits many venial sins. Then he is much engrossed with things of time; much preoccupied with the affairs of daily life. In a word, he is a man of ordinary virtue—one of the masses; an average Catholic, living for God, but not at all indifferent to the opinions of men; determined to please God, yet not by any means inclined to despise the favor and the smile of the world. He is one who dreads mortal sin, but who is not likely to distress himself much about lesser faults.

Such a man is no Saint; indeed, he makes no pretensions to sanctity; he does not profess to be a model; he is a traveller wending his way along the dusty road of life; his feet are bruised with many a stone, and torn and gashed with many a brier. At last he reaches the end of his journey; sickness comes, and his term of trial is nearly over. He lies on the bed of death, his end approaches; at last he dies he dies as men generally die, that is to say, *as he lived*. His death is, in fact, what deaths almost invariably are, an abridgment, an epitome of life: it is good, not perfect. We rejoice that it is no worse, though we might wish it were better; it inspires us with confidence and hope, but it is not the death of a Saint.

Here I have sketched, as though with a few hasty strokes of the pencil, a typical man. One who may be said to represent a considerable number. In fact (if we confine our thoughts to Catholics), it probably covers the majority of cases. We ourselves must surely come under the number, for if we dare not aspire to the innocence of a St. John the Baptist, so neither shall we consent to take our stand among the reprobate. Indeed, we may say that this class is made up of myriads. But now the question arises: What is to become of these myriads? Where are we to place men such as the one whose character I have roughly drawn?

Were we Protestants of the ordinary type, we should be sorely perplexed, for they permit only Heaven and Hell, and he is as little fitted for the one place as for the other. They place us in a most awkward dilemma so long as they allow us but the two alternatives.

Is he, then, to be borne straight to Heaven, without any previous purification, without any cleansing or preparation? Is this soul—the abode of a thousand imperfections and small vices and failings—to take its stand at once among the glorious citizens of the City of God? Certainly not! The words of the Holy Spirit Himself are eminently explicit on this point. God declares, in unmistakable language, that "Nothing defiled shall enter Heaven." (Cf. *Apoc.* 21:27). *Nothing* defiled. No! Not a stain or a blot, be it but of a sin of thought, or a hasty word, however passing, however momentary; if but a particle of earthly dust or defilement still adhere to the soul, it may not, it cannot enter.

No one who reflects upon what Heaven is would allow for a moment that an ordinary average Christian can enter at once into its possession. For what *is* Heaven in its essence and substance? What constitutes the ecstatic joys of Heaven? What do we mean by Heaven?

Heaven is the inseparable union of God the infinite Creator with man, His fragile and lowly creature. It is the union between God and the soul. What this union is we can neither imagine nor describe. "Eye hath not seen it, ear hath not heard it, the heart cannot fathom it, words cannot picture it, the mind cannot conceive it." All we know is that in it consists the essential bliss of Heaven—a bliss so excessive, so overpowering, that without it all other joys are empty, illusory and unsatisfying.

Now, who will dare say that God would so unite with Himself any soul not perfectly spotless? Who will assert that Infinite Purity and Holiness would extend His arms and draw to His side and press to His bosom anything that is defiled, or stained, or sinful, or impure? He knows little of God who imagines that there can be any such union between light and darkness, between truth and falsehood, beauty and deformity.

Then, must we say that all these souls are to be condemned to the quenchless flames of Hell? Are all but the very highest of the canonized Saints to pass their eternity in the prison house of God's wrath? Are all but a solitary Saint here and there to be cast away utterly? This is the awful conclusion to which a rejection of Purgatory must inevitably lead us. For reason itself rebels at the notion of the imperfect being admitted to the embraces of God; our whole sense of God's inaccessible purity and holiness is shocked at the very suggestion of such a union. We may not, we cannot, entertain it. So that *if* Hell be the only alternative, to Hell they must go; if the bottomless pit be the only other abode, *then* that must be their dwelling place for ever and ever.

Ah, what a doctrine! A doctrine to freeze the blood in one's veins; a doctrine without reason as it is without love. The fruit of the tree of heresy is indeed bitter.

How different is the sound Catholic doctrine of Purgatory! It neither outrages God's holiness, on the one hand, by sending sinners directly into His presence, nor His mercy, on the other hand, by ejecting them directly into Hell. It appears to me that this doctrine rejected, scorned, derided though it be by heretics, reveals to us much of the grandeur and majesty of God, and illuminates in a marvellous manner the hidden depths of His Divine perfections. Any (so-called) religious body rejecting the doctrine of Purgatory turns out of court one of the most eloquent witnesses to the personal loveliness and perfection of God, and destroys one of the most striking arguments in proof of His infinite sanctity and beauty.

(RIGHT REV. MONSIGNOR JOHN S. VAUGHAN)*

St. Philip Neri had a very tender devotion for the souls in Purgatory. His great attraction was to pray for those whose consciences he had directed during life. In his opinion, a father's charity ought to follow them to eternity, because

---

* The above extract has been copied by kind permission of the Author from his valuable work, *Thoughts for All Times.*

real charity, says St. Paul, never falleth away. He avowed that many of his spiritual children appeared to him after their death to request his prayers or to thank him for those he had said in their favor.

We are also assured by him that he obtained by the aid of these Poor Souls very many graces. He himself appeared to a holy religious crowned with glory in the midst of a beautiful procession. The religious, encouraged by the friendly and meek air with which the Saint regarded him, asked who were the happy beings that surrounded him. St. Philip answered they were the souls whom he had helped during his life in this world, and who had been delivered from Purgatory by his prayers. He added that they had met him at his death and introduced him into the kingdom of the blessed.

◈ TWENTY-FIFTH DAY ◈

A Day of Prayer for Souls Who while on Earth Were Most Devoted to the Sacred Passion

LET us today, with sentiments of fervent piety, make an offering of the merits of Christ's sufferings in behalf of those who were most devoted to His Sacred Passion.

The Adorable Sacrifice of the Mass is the most efficacious means of relieving the Holy Souls. All Catholics know that in that Sacrifice the merits of the Sacrifice of the Cross are offered to the Eternal Father, and that it thus presents to Him a satisfaction in itself infinitely greater than any debt which those souls can owe to His Divine justice. These Holy Souls are a part of the Church, and when her priests are ordained they receive the power of offering the Sacrifice for the living and the dead. St. Anthony of Padua, in his sermon, *In Cæna Domini*, tells us that the division of the Sacred Host into three parts, which is made by the priest before his Communion, signifies the three parts of the Church, the blessed in Heaven, the living on earth, and the dead; and St. Thomas adds that the Mass has a threefold effect: forgiving sins in this world, alleviating pain in Purgatory, and increasing glory in Heaven. Many texts and figures in Holy Scripture are applied in this meaning by the Fathers and Saints.

Theologians tell us that the temporal punishment due to sin is directly remitted by the Holy Sacrifice, and that this is the tradition of the Apostles. They tell us that this Sacrifice is the most powerful means of all that we possess for satisfaction, as the Council of Trent lays down that the souls in Purgatory are helped by the suffrages of the Faithful, "but chiefly by the acceptable Sacrifice of the Altar." Indeed, the chief fruit of the Holy Sacrifice is said to be that of satisfaction; "for, as sacrifice, especially that of the Cross, has the power given to it of satisfying for the punishment due to our sins, so this unbloody Sacrifice, which is a living image of that Bloody Sacrifice, is properly and directly instituted for the application to us *ex opere operato* of the fruit of satisfaction, so that, as they say in the schools, what is done in that first Sacrifice by way of sufficiency is wrought in this other by way of efficiency." Again, some great theologians hold that the application of the satisfaction which is derived from this Sacrifice benefits the holy dead *ex opere operato*, and by a law of justice; while other things, such as indulgences, and the application of our good works, benefit them by way of suffrage—that is, out of the mercy and liberality of God, who accepts them for that purpose. An argument for this opinion is based on the words of Ordination above mentioned, and on the statements of Councils and Fathers, that the Adorable Sacrifice is to be offered for the dead in the same way as for the living.

The lives of the Saints are very full of anecdotes which illustrate the efficacy of the Sacrifice of the Altar for the relief of the Holy Souls. It may be useful to give here some of the reasons, which are found in various writers, for the Christian custom of celebrating Mass on certain special days for those who are departed. Five Masses may be said to be almost prescribed by that custom when there is nothing to prevent them—that is, on the day of burial, on the third, seventh, and thirtieth days after death, and on the anniversary. In many parts of the Church it has been the rule never to let any Christian be buried without the celebration of Mass. The Mass of the third day is mentioned in the Clementine Constitutions, and it is said to represent the Resurrection of Our Lord on the third day, or the restoration in the soul of the image of the Ever-Blessed Trinity, or the threefold purification of thoughts, words, and deeds. The Mass of the seventh day is significant of the eternal Sabbath or rest of the holy dead. We find a connection between seven days and the length of mourning in the Old Testament, as in the case of Joseph mourning for Jacob. The thirtieth day is said to be chosen, as that was the number of days during which the Israelites mourned for Moses, or for the mystical reason that Our Lord was thirty when He was baptized, or that thirty is the full-grown age of man, in which, it is said, we are all to rise again. The institution of anniversaries is traced by some up to the time of the Apostles, and it is so natural and universal as to need no explanation.

There are many questions which have arisen as to Masses for the dead, on account of the great frequency of such Masses and the various circumstances which may attend their celebration. Thus, although a Solemn Mass, with all its ceremonies and accompaniments, is in itself of no greater intrinsic merit than a simple Low Mass, still the Church encourages the practice of celebrating the former, which may cause greater devotion, and so greater benefit to the soul for whom it is offered. Again, it is clear that a Mass of *Requiem*, in which all the prayers have a distinct reference to the relief of the dead, on that account profits them more than another Mass, although the intrinsic value of the sacrifice is the same in each case. Again, it must be clear that a Mass celebrated at a privileged altar* is more directly and powerfully beneficial to a soul in Purgatory than another, and that, if the words of the concession of the privilege require that it should be a Mass of *Requiem*, such a Mass alone will gain the indulgence.

It may also be well to remember that to hear Mass for the holy dead is an act of religion and devotion which is certain to benefit them very much. This is a great incentive to the hearing of as many Masses as possible, and with the special intention of hearing them for the Holy Souls. In this way those who are not priests may in some sort share their power as to helping those in Purgatory, and those who are too poor to be able to procure Masses for them may be able to supply the effect of their poverty by hearing many Masses for them. It is certain that to hear Mass is a very high act of religion, next to that of saying Mass; and that those who hear Mass do in truth offer it, according to their power, to the Eternal Father, which is the most excellent act of worship that can be performed. The priest in the Mass, when he turns to the people at the *Orate fratres*, calls it "my and your sacrifice," and the hearers, therefore, honor God by offering that Holy Sacrifice as well as the priest. Suarez says that as the oblation of this Sacrifice is fruitful in the way of satisfaction and impetration *ex opere operato*, all those who offer it, and therefore those who hear it, receive its benefits in the same way, and not only in proportion to their own devotion. This is not certain, because, as other theologians say, the satisfactory fruit of the Adorable Sacrifice is received by the priest alone, who alone offers it in the name of Christ. But, at all events, the fruit of impetration, as it is called, belongs to the hearers also, inasmuch as the priest, in the name of Christ, offers the sacrifice for all, and

---

* The designation of *privileged altar* was abolished in the Apostolic Constitution "The Doctrine of Indulgences" of Pope Paul VI, January 1, 1967, in which it is stated that the Church "has decided that suffrages be applied to them [the Poor Souls] to the widest possible extent at any Sacrifice of the Mass whatsoever, abolishing all special privileges in this regard." —*Publisher*, 2005.

more especially for those who are present. This fruit may be applied by them for the benefit of the Holy Souls for whom they may hear Mass.

These are more or less theological considerations on which Christian piety may feed itself, and which may be made the solid foundation of a great amount of practical devotion. A Mass heard every day for the special intention of relieving the Holy Souls may be, in many cases, not only a daily alms of immense value to those sufferers who are so dear to Our Lord, but also the source of immense benefits and great protection to ourselves, not only from its own intrinsic efficacy, but also on account of the numberless prayers which we may thus win from those for whom we perform this most blessed act of religion.

—REV. H. J. COLERIDGE, S.J.

━━━━━━

The pious exercise of the Stations of the Cross is a continued meditation on the Passion of Our Lord. To it innumerable indulgences have been annexed by the Sovereign Pontiffs, even the same as those of the *Via Crucis* in Jerusalem, or other places of the Holy Land, whence it appears how profitable this exercise must be to the Holy Souls. We read in the life of the Venerable Mary of Antigua that a nun of her convent, having died, appeared to her and said: "Why is it that you do not offer for me and for the other souls the Stations of the Cross?" The servant of God remained in suspense at these words, when she heard Our Lord say to her: "The exercise of the Way of the Cross is so profitable to the souls in Purgatory that this soul has come to ask it of you in the name of all. The *Via Crucis* is a suffrage of great importance for these souls. By offering it for them you will have them as so many protectors, who will pray for you and defend your cause before My justice. Tell your sisters to rejoice in this treasure and the precious capital they have in it, that they may profit by it."

━━━━━━

The exercises of a Mission were given in a parish; the Faithful went in crowds to hear the word of God and obtain the pardon of their sins. Three men only refused obstinately to profit by the grace offered them. They had promised each other and sworn not to enter the Church, and especially not to go to Confession. The wife of one of them went one day to the missionary and confided to him her grief. "Have you children?" asked the priest. "Yes, Father," she replied, "I have two, still young." "Well," he said, "bring them to the Church, make devoutly with them the Stations of the Cross for the Poor Souls in Purgatory, and ask, through the intercession of those souls that you shall have relieved, the conversion of your husband, and I am sure that you will obtain it. Be certain of two things: that the exercise of the Way of the Cross is one of the most efficacious means to relieve the souls in Purgatory, and that it is equally efficacious to obtain by their intercession the succor that we need."

Every day at twelve o'clock, when the church was empty, the virtuous woman went to kneel before the tabernacle with her two little children, and afterwards made with them the Stations of the Cross for the intentions indicated by the pious missionary. On the eve of the last day of the mission, the sinner knelt repentant at the feet of the priest, and next day had the happiness of receiving Holy Communion at his wife's side. After the Mass he pressed to his heart and blessed his two children.

TWENTY-SIXTH DAY

A Day of Prayer for Souls Suffering for Attachment to Earthly Things

MANY souls are suffering in Purgatory for having been too much attached to earthly possessions. Offer for their relief some indulgenced prayers.

Catholic doctrine declares that souls who depart this life with the stain of venial sin, or with forgiven mortal sins not fully atoned for, are detained for a season—for a longer or shorter period, according to their guilt—in the flames of Purgatory, where they are cleansed from every defilement and every spot, and prepared for Heaven. There they suffer the pangs of ungratified desire; there they are desolate with grief because their sojourn is prolonged; there they are grievously afflicted because He who is to be their "reward exceeding great" is far from them, and they are shut out and deprived for a time of their inheritance and portion in the land of the living. They thirst after Him whom their souls love as the parched land thirsts for the autumn rains; they long for Him as the weary traveller longs for refreshment and shade; they pine for His possession as a mother pines for her lost and only son; they are sick with grief as the bride when the bridegroom tarries. Ah! Who will describe their anguish, who will express their bitterness? Their love is the measure of their distress, and, in so far as a finite nature will permit, their love is proportioned to its object; and its object is the Infinite God—God the unlimited, the boundless, the only absolute beauty. To measure their grief, then, we must measure God's loveliness; to gauge the depth of their pain we must sound the bottomless abyss of God's perfections. But who can do this? Let it suffice, then, to say that their pains are beyond all computation, and exceed all thought and power of utterance. Such is the doctrine of the Church of Christ.

What a perfect flood of light it casts over the being of God! Into what startling relief it brings out the dazzling brightness of His purity, which cannot suffer a sin-stained soul to approach it! How wondrously it reveals His hatred of sin and His abhorrence of all defilement! How it lights up, in a word, the whole position of God, and points to Him as the center and circumference, the beginning and end, the Alpha and Omega, of all things! All things become desirable or undesirable, pleasant or unpleasant, good or bad, merely as related to Him. His attitude determines and regulates all things, gives to them their fairness and attractions, clothes them with grace and beauty, and makes them what they are.

So soon as the soul has shuffled off its mortal coil it finds itself, so to speak, within the circle of God's attraction. It is impelled toward Him with the utmost violence, as the meteor is impelled toward the earth. What now happens? There may be no grievous sin to raise an impenetrable obstacle—a wall of brass—between it and God. Nevertheless, if there be but venial sins, or the slightest failing, imperfections light as air, they will act upon it as the atmosphere upon the meteor—*i.e.*, check it, retard it, impede and interfere with its union with God, till in its anguish the soul burns and wastes away with unsatisfied desires until every trace of sin is destroyed.

If but once opened to the beatific vision, even but for one brief moment, the eyes of the soul can never close again without inexpressible pain. To close them and shut out that vision is agony. Not one instant's enjoyment of the sight of God can be forfeited without the acutest suffering. On this earth we may consent to live on without seeing God; but this is solely because we have *never* seen Him. Once see God, then to live any longer without seeing Him is impossible; for such a one all true life has ended. The soul may yet exist—it *must* exist—but it is only in the throes of death. Eternal death is, in fact, nothing more than the eternal closing of the eyes upon the vision of God. Hence the eternal darkness. Hence, too, the unending death. Such is Hell.

On the other hand, so long as the eyes may yet hope one day to see, the soul is only in Purgatory. The thought of that longed-for moment sustains it. Yet each successive instant that must first elapse flows by as an unmeasured sea of bitterness and grief. Yes; for to be restrained when we would feast on the glory of the Infinite is to suffer the pangs of an inconceivable hunger. The pains of sense, even of hell itself, are light and easy to support *compared to that*. Nothing but that seems quite unendurable. Ah, God! Thou art verily our all. *Deus meus et omnia*. Without Thee, all else is nothing. If

Thou smile upon us, our joy overflows and drowns all care and sorrow. Hide Thy countenance for a moment, and we are troubled. Cast us off utterly, and we wither away.

What is Heaven itself? God securely possessed. What is Hell? God eternally lost. And what is Purgatory? God hidden—hidden for a time, as the sun is hidden by the passing clouds. When God is thus hidden, then the soul is deprived of light and warmth and beauty and comeliness, as the earth is deprived of beauty when night lies thick over mountain, plain and valley.

We may aid our suffering brethren by our prayers and sacrifices. These imprisoned souls are no strangers to us, but most dear and honored friends. Heresy, thank God, has built up no impassable barrier between *us* and those we once knew and loved, and who have now passed away. They are still our friends—yea, more our friends than ever—and we may still extend toward them a helping hand in the hour of their trial. Let us hearken to their cry, "Have pity on me, at least you, my friends!" and do our best to succour them.

—RIGHT REV. MONSIGNOR JOHN S. VAUGHAN*

The following story showing the interest taken by the Holy Souls in those whom they loved on earth was related by the Rev. Father Schröder in a sermon he preached in the cathedral at Munich, and he said he had the details from the priest to whom it occurred.

Late on a stormy evening a priest of one of the parish churches of Vienna opened the door himself on hearing a loud ring at his door. A lady entered, saying she had been sent to require his immediate attendance for a gentleman in danger of death, adding that the distance was considerable, and begging he would take the Holy Viaticum. As soon as the priest was ready she accompanied him to the parish Church to procure the Blessed Sacrament, and said she

---

* Copied by kind permission of the Author from his instructive book, *Thoughts for All Times.*

would go before to show him the way. The night was wild, and before they had reached their destination, a house in the suburbs, a hurricane was blowing, and the snowstorm was terrific. The lady stopped, saying, "This is the gentleman's house," and she rang the bell. As the door was not opened, she did so a second time. On looking round, the priest found she was gone.

Then the window was opened, and an elderly gentleman called out to know what was wanted. The priest answered that he had been hurriedly sent for to attend a dying man. "There is no dying man in this house," the gentleman answered, "and no one sick. It is quite a mistake"; and he was about to close the window, when, moved by a natural feeling of compassion for the poor priest, who could scarcely stand, he added: "But if you would like to take shelter till the storm is past, you are welcome." So he opened the door and showed him into a sitting-room, and set his lamp down on a table. He then threw open a door at the other end of the room and disclosed a small oratory, in which there was an altar, a large image of Our Blessed Lady, and a lamp burning before it, saying, "There you can deposit your burden." The priest placed the Blessed Sacrament on the altar, lighted two candles, made his genuflection, and re-entered the room, saying, "I am sorry to have disturbed you, but at least I see the mistake has brought me to the house of a good Catholic." "There you are entirely mistaken," replied the gentleman; "I am an unbeliever, and glory in so being. No doubt you are astonished at finding a chapel and an altar and lamp burning, but if you like—and it is impossible to attempt returning during this whirlwind—I shall explain the meaning."

He then told the priest that his mother, on her deathbed, had made him promise to keep that lamp burning as long as he lived; that in that oratory she had daily prayed; and that he, when a child, had knelt with her. Then he spoke eloquently in praise of his mother—told of her goodness, her piety, her love of the poor, her only fault being her attachment to the Catholic Faith, which he excused as an illusion which had done no harm to anyone, and made her happy. Probably for many years he had never spoken of his mother to his own associates, but to this stranger, whom it was likely he would never see again, he poured out his whole heart, and seemed to take a strange delight in recording all his mother's excellence and her love for him; how she always said, "Hans, my son, I shall never cease begging Our Lady for your conversion"; and when dying she said that, when in the presence of God, it would be her first prayer that he might return to the Faith.

The priest, well versed in the science of souls, questioned him, and lured him on to talk. He told him how he had once been a good Catholic; how he had discovered that religion was all nonsense; what a life he had then led; how he had grieved his mother, for which he was sorry, adding that the least he could do was to remain faithful to his promise; and though he never looked at the altar, he took care the lamp should be kept burning all through these years, for she had been long dead. He suddenly arose, took the lamp, and said, "See, here you may see her portrait!" and held the light up to a large oil painting, which the priest instantly recognized as the portrait of the lady who had conducted him to the house. Feeling that a supernatural mystery was being enacted, he concealed his emotion, and continued encouraging him to speak more and more.

The night wore on, the hurricane ceased, neither seemed to heed it, and, to bring the story to a close, by three o'clock the penitent was kneeling at the priest's feet, bathed in tears, making a full confession of his whole life, and in such good dispositions that the priest gave him then and there Holy Communion at his mother's little altar. They stayed some time longer together, and before dawn the priest took leave, promising to return on the following day and pay him a visit. He kept his word, but on arriving at the house he heard that the gentleman had died. He had been found dead in his bed that morning. We may suppose the priest thanked God very fervently for the wonderful grace He had granted that soul.

∾ TWENTY-SEVENTH DAY ∾

A Day of Prayer for Those Who Were Members Of Pious Confraternities and Sodalities

T HE Holy Souls may be considered, in one respect, as the choicest and dearest of Mary's children, except the Saints themselves, who need nothing and are deprived of nothing. She has been made in a particular manner their Mother by Our Lord on the Cross, for in them the fruits of His Precious Blood are secured. More especially may we consider her interested in those who while on earth made special profession of honoring her. The lives of the Saints, the chronicles of religious Orders, and other such records, are full of anecdotes and revelations, which all tend to prove that Our Lady is constantly exercising her power in favor of the Holy Souls; and that, on the other hand, devotions that are practiced in her especial honor are among the most efficacious means which the children of the Church on earth possess of helping those blessed sufferers.

Devout writers tell us that, after the Holy Sacrifice of the Mass, the Rosary is the most powerful weapon that can be used to obtain their deliverance. The Holy Rosary stands, to the great mass of Christians, much in the same place as the Divine Office of the Church to those who are bound to recite it, or who have the custom of so doing. The Divine Office is the great public prayer of the Catholic Church, and it remains such even in the case of those who do not recite it in the choir, but privately and singly. And it has great efficacy on that account, for in the Catholic Church there is a special power and blessing on united, universal, and, as it were, official prayer and praise, which cannot be altogether impaired even by the unworthiness of some who are the ministers of the Church for this purpose. The Holy Rosary is sometimes called the Psalter of the Blessed Virgin, and the universality of its use renders it, in a sense, the prayer of the whole Church, though not in the same degree as the Divine Office. Intrinsically, moreover, it has an immense impetratory power with God, because it is, in fact, the pleading before Him of the merits of Our Lord and of Our Blessed Lady in all the mysteries which it commemorates, and which embrace the whole range of the scheme of our Redemption as accomplished by Him. Then, again, it pleads all these merits, as it were, through the heart and through the lips of Mary herself, and so it adds to the power of the mysteries in themselves that of her perfect prayer and intercession, and the affections and intensity of charity which glow in her bosom. Again, it uses, with all its marvellous power, the words of Our Blessed Lord in the *Pater Noster,* and of the Archangel, St. Elizabeth, and the Church in the *Ave Maria*, being also at the same time a chain of most excellent acts of faith, hope, charity, and other supernatural virtues, which are exercised in the consideration of the mysteries.

It would be almost impossible to exaggerate the importance which holy writers attach to the practice of this devotion, whether as a means of intercession for the Holy Souls or for our own benefit, for in this, as in many other cases, the charity which we practice toward them flows back in abundant streams to the benefit of ourselves in this world and in the next. The various forms which devotion to Our Blessed Lady may take are almost innumerable. Masses in her honor, Masses offered for the souls devout to her, or to whom she may wish to apply them, alms given or works of mercy practiced with the same intention; or, again, the recital of her Office, the visiting her statues, honoring her pictures, and the like, may all be used for the benefit of the Holy Souls.   —REV. H. J. COLERIDGE, S.J.

Among the sorrows of kind hearts there is one which seems as if it grew greater in each succeeding generation of the world. It is the enormous growth of poverty and wretchedness, and our own inability to relieve it. There is hardly one among us who has not felt this. So overwhelming is the misery, that those who have little to give feel the pain as much as those who have nothing, and those who have much to give almost more. For giving opens a man's heart, and makes him love to give, and those who have much to give know best how little it is compared with the necessity. Yet this yearning to give alms comes from the Sacred Heart of Jesus, and it must be satisfied; and how can we better satisfy it than by giving alms to those who need it most—the Holy Souls in Purgatory? We can all do this; and how much might we do, even for our dear poor on earth, if we commended their cause to the souls whom God allows us to liberate, and make a sweet bargain with them that, when once in the free air of Heaven, their first homage and salutation over, they should pray for an abundant outpouring of grace upon rich men, that their hearts might be opened, like the hearts of the first Christians, to deny themselves and to feast the poor of Christ!   —FATHER FABER

OUR HOLY DEAD

Twilight—glad Day's departing kiss of peace—
Yet lingered softly in the convent gladon,
And Nature seemed to hush her beating heart,
A-listening breathless for Night's stealing tread.
A golden glory still illumed the west,
As though the sun cast eager glances back
To catch a glimpse of star-crowned, queenly Night,
And smile a welcome to her peaceful reign
The flowers that all day long had gazed on Heaven,
And sent their grateful odors to the sun—
In mute thanksgiving for the tints they wore—
Now closed their petals, and in slumber slept,
While gentle zephyrs lulled them sweet to rest,
And Angel dewdrops kissed them, every one.
At such an hour, when restless thoughts give place
To calm and holy musings, and the soul—
Still yearning for the peace serene, that reigned
In Eden, till rebellious sin disturbed

The harmony of Nature with her Lord—
Is raised above the petty things of time,
And holds communion with a higher world.
At such an hour, alone, I pensive stood
Within the holy relic-ground, where sleep
Another sisterhood, whose toils are o'er;
Whose hands are folded in a still repose;
Whose feet, once wearied with the daily round
Of constant duty, may now rest for aye.
Methought, if all these sleepers could awake,
And stand around me in the shadows dim,
What solemn words of counsel would be heard!
What sweet encouragement would they not give
To live for God alone, and do His Will!
What earnest pleadings for the souls still bound
In penal fires, awaiting bright release!
But no! they will not rise; and yet they speak.
Within my soul I hear their voices plead;
Out of the depths they come to crave our prayers.
A Miserere psalm floats soft around,
And melts away my heart to tears. But what of that?
What matters it, though loving eyes may weep?
What matters it, though loving hands may strew
The fairest flowers upon the pulseless hearts,
Or raise a monument of marble rare,
And trace the epitaph with ceaseless tears?
All this consoles the living—not the dead.
Ah, me! how much fond love lies in the grave!
How many hopes are covered 'neath the sod!
How many bleeding hearts are living down
E'en in the silent tomb for weary years!
But, oh! how sadly few the prayers that rise
From Earth to Heaven for those who've passed away!
Too few! too few! And yet we loved them well!
And promised oft that Time's cold hand should ne'er
Blot out their mem'ry from our faithful hearts;
Although dead years should lie in piles between
Their parting from us, and our joining them,

That never, never should they be forgot!
Had heart deceived the head? or fancy fond
Beguiled us into dreaming that a tear
Would prove to those long gone we'd kept our pledge?
Ah, no! the dead will only feel that we
Are true to them—by all the prayers we say.

*   *   *   *   *

The gloaming deepened, and the stars looked down
Like Angels watching o'er the holy ground;
I turned me toward the Temple, where God's love
Keeps Him a captive bound. The while I thought,
If souls thus vowed to God, who lived for Him,
And died so full of peace, and rest so sweet,
May yet be passing through all-cleansing fires,
Ere they can take a place 'mid Angel bands,
And walk where lily feet alone may tread—
The Lamb to follow whereso'er He goes—
What must it be for those who've trailed the robe,
Once made so pure and white at sacred Font,
Along the sin-strewn way of earthly life,
Where worldly cares obscure the final end?
"Miseremini mei!" Will not their wail
Our dull hearts touch, and waken lively faith?

*   *   *   *   *

Ah! ye who mourn some beloved dead,
Remember well what only can avail
The souls departed to the Shadow Land;
Let sacrifice for such be duly made:
Let pious offerings to high Heaven plead;
Let prayers and alms your faithfulness attest;
'Tis thus your love will soar above the tomb,
And weave a wreath to crown your holy Dead.

Benedict XIII, in his *Trigesimi*, in order to show how much
assistance the prayer, *"Requiescant in pace"* [see p. 159], is to
the souls in Purgatory, recounts a wonderful instance which
is related in the chronicles of the Chartreuse.

An English gentleman having lately passed to a better life, his son went to visit the Fathers of Chartreuse to recommend to their prayers the soul of the deceased, giving them a large quantity of gold as alms. The monks having been all assembled by the Prior, and the soul of the good knight having been recommended to their suffrages, they chanted all together, *"Requiescat in pace,"** and returned in silence to their cells. The pious almsgiver was astonished, and thinking the suffrage the Prior had ordered too little, he said to him: "Reverend Father, is this very short prayer of the friars all that my father's soul is to have? Are you not going to add anything more?" The Prior, having called the monks back, ordered every one to write upon a small piece of paper his *"Requiescat in pace."* He then sent for a scales, and had the mass of gold placed on one side of the balance and on the other the little pieces of paper, and behold! most wonderful to relate, the gold, though very heavy, mounted up on high as if it were a feather, while the pieces of paper sank low down with the holy weight of their words. This prodigy, which drew tears from the eyes of the almsgiver, should move us to send frequently and with devotion for the souls in Purgatory this joyous message, *"Requiescant in pace."**

⤳ TWENTY-EIGHTH DAY ⤳

A Day of Fervor to Atone for Souls Suffering For Negligence in Spiritual Duties

SUCH are our weakness and extreme misery that they appear even in our best actions. Yet these will be examined with strict scrutiny. The Lord declares him "accursed who does His work negligently." What a dreadful

---

* *Requiescat in pace* = "May he (or she) rest in peace." *Requiescant in pace* = "May they rest in peace." —*Publisher*, 2005.

thing to appear before Him with imperfect works!—prayers said without devotion, the Divine Office recited with distraction, meditations made without fruit. Let us pray today for those who are suffering for such offenses.

In suffering there is something sadder than suffering itself—abandonment. To suffer and find someone to sympathize, to be interested, to compassionate—this is not the saddest suffering; but to suffer, and realize that no one shares our suffering by a sentiment, a thought, or a tear; to suffer, and find no consolation—this is torture multiplied by torture. This it was that drew from Job, seated in his misery, and from Jeremias, weeping over the ruins of Jerusalem, their most mournful lamentation: "I sought a consoler, and I found none." And this it is that gives the sorrows of Purgatory a sovereign interest; the sorrows of the souls there are the most forsaken of all sorrows; they can truly say in the terrible reality of their abandonment: "They have heard the voice of my groaning, and among them there is no one to console me."

Have you ever reflected on this phenomenon, so desolating for our dear deceased brethren, so humiliating for us— forgetfulness of the dead? For myself, I confess it often inspires me with the gravest and most sorrowful thoughts. When I reflect on the place which the dead hold in the memory of the living, I can but say: Is it possible we shall so soon be forgotten? Alas! We vainly seek to deceive ourselves on this point; forgetfulness is the sad inheritance which our life bequeaths to our death. When the face of man disappears from our sight, his memory passes swiftly from our mind—so swiftly that we forget even those we loved the most. This forgetfulness we cannot believe when the last farewell has been said, and our soul, overwhelmed with sorrow, promises itself a consolation in immortal remembrance. But, alas, for this poor heart of ours, all things pass from it—all, even to the sentiments which form its individual life! While the stroke of death still rings in our ears, and our heart bleeds from the recent wounds it inflicted, we remember. But time marches on; a few steps, the remembrance and the sorrow begin to grow faint; the train of life brings other relations and new affections. Time still marches on, and we dream of a new existence where the dead will be no more needed; a step farther—and already we are quite accustomed to do without them!

Sometimes the grass has not grown over our grave, and already new friendships take root in the hearts that so bitterly regretted us, effacing little by little all memories of us until they finally disappear forever. Around your last sigh, perhaps, there will be the sound of regrets and praises, but as the strokes of the bell which tolls your requiem grow fainter and fainter in the distance until lost in silence, so your life will soon be heard of no more. While our bodies, crumbling to dust, are confounded with a thousand other things already pulverized, our memory little by little is confounded with the forgotten generations; then complete silence, and of all the sounds that come borne on the winds of Heaven there will not be one to tell that we ever existed. Silence everywhere! Even in the little corner of the world where we passed our lives the same silence reigns. *Even there* your name will no longer fall upon the ear; never more will it excite the interest of your survivors, or enter into their conversations. Oh, how true are the words of the *Imitation:* "Trust not in thy friends and kinsfolk, nor put off the welfare of thy soul to hereafter, for men will sooner forget thee than thou imaginest. It is better now to provide in time, and send some good before thee, than to trust to others helping thee after thy death. If thou are not now careful for thyself, who will be careful for thee hereafter?"

I know there are some exceptions to the universality of this forgetfulness. We meet hearts carrying an ever-bleeding wound and remembrance, a regret that cannot die, who make the sorrow itself a protection for the cherished memory, but truth forces us to say that these are the exceptions. But there is one heart on earth which never forgets, which ever remembers, and prays without ceasing—a heart ready every hour to come to the aid of the abandoned dead: it is the heart of the Catholic Church. She is the Mother of the children who combat on earth, Mother also of her children who suffer in Purgatory, and the lamentations of the one and the other ever find an echo in her compassionate heart. During this month especially she says to her desolate ones in Purgatory: "Be consoled, my children, be consoled. If your friends no longer pray for you, if you are forgotten by all, I will always pray for you, I will not forget you. I am your Mother, and I will call your brothers and sisters into my House, that they may obtain, by their prayers and merits, solace for you in your sufferings, and may hasten the day of your deliverance."

Thus does the holy Church console her afflicted children.

—FATHER FELIX, S.J.

We read in the *Life of St. Elizabeth of Portugal* that after the death of her daughter Constance she learned the pitiful state of the deceased in Purgatory. The young Princess had been married but a short time previous to the King of Castile, when she was snatched away by sudden death from the affection of her family and her subjects. Elizabeth had just received these tidings, and set out with the King, her husband, for the city of Santarem, when a hermit, coming forth from his solitude, ran after the royal cortège, crying that he wished to speak to the Queen.

As soon as he came into her presence, he related that more than once, while he was praying in his hermitage, the Princess had appeared to him, urgently entreating him to make known to her mother that she was languishing in the depths of Purgatory, that she was condemned to long and terrible suffering, but that she would be delivered if for the space of a year the Holy Sacrifice of the Mass was celebrated for her every day. Elizabeth turned to the King and asked what he thought of this communication. "I believe," he replied, "that it is wise to do what has been pointed out to you in so extraordinary a manner. After all, to have

Masses celebrated for our dear child is nothing more than a duty." A holy priest, Ferdinand Mendez, was appointed to say the Masses.

At the end of the year, Constance appeared to St. Elizabeth, clad in a brilliant white robe. "Today, dear Mother," said she, "I am delivered from the pains of Purgatory, and am about to enter Heaven." Filled with consolation and joy, the Saint went to the church to return thanks to God. There she found the priest Mendez, who assured her that on the previous day he had finished the celebration of the three hundred and sixty-five Masses with which he had been charged. The Queen then understood that God had kept the promise which He had made to the pious hermit, and she testified her gratitude by distributing abundant alms to the poor.

⌒ TWENTY-NINTH DAY ⌒

A Day of Prayer for Souls Nearest to Being Released

THERE are many souls in Purgatory who only await a very trifling suffrage on our part to obtain admittance into Heaven. Let us be very fervent in our supplications for them today.

———

St. Paul says of the Holy Angels that they are "all ministering spirits, sent to minister to them who shall receive the inheritance of salvation." These few words are enough to remind us of their relations to the Holy Souls. The ministering of the Angels begins with our entrance into the world, and, as the Apostle implies, is not to cease until we receive "the inheritance of salvation." How faithfully and lovingly they watch over us as long as our period of trial lasts no tongue can tell, and it will be one of the great surprises of the next world to learn. It is certain also that the care of the Angels increases in vigilance, if that be possible, as the last moment of life draws nigh; that they are standing by us in our last conflict; and that they meet us at our entrance into the next world, conveying our soul to the tribunal of the Judge, or, rather, as that judgment takes place at the moment of death, being present while it is being made. The Angels rejoice immensely at a good and happy death. The Church bids her ministers commend the soul as it departs to their charge. "When thy soul shall depart from thy body, may the resplendent multitude of the Angels meet thee, may the court of the Apostles receive thee," and the rest. And again: "Come to his assistance, all ye Saints of God; meet him, all ye Angels of God, receiving his soul and offering it in the sight of the Most High. May Christ receive thee who hath called thee, and may the Angels conduct thee to Abraham's bosom."

The Angels stand by at the time of judgment and defend the soul against the charges of the devils, as is found in many of the revelations of the Saints. If the soul be sentenced to Purgatory, the Angels conduct it thither, as St. Thomas teaches; and Suarez says that this escorting of the souls to their place of exile is to comfort them, and also to show them honor as the children of God and spouses of Christ. But when the souls are once conveyed to Purgatory, we are told that the Angels, especially their Guardian Angels, visit them and console them frequently. The full enjoyment of the society of the Angels cannot be had until we reach Heaven; but they are not prevented from comforting the Suffering Souls in their prison, any more than from suggesting to the living to pray for them and offer for them works of satisfaction or the Holy Sacrifice of the Mass.

It may be thought that the mere presence of such blessed and glorious beings, which must be far more keenly perceived by the souls separated from the body than is now possible to us, would go far to make the mournful prison of Purgatory bright and joyous with the light of Heaven itself. But we cannot tell to what extent the Holy Souls are allowed to enjoy the natural effects of the near presence of the Angels. We may feel certain, however, that their visits are of ineffable comfort and relief. We may take as an image of this consolation that visit which Our Lord condescended to receive from one of the Angels in His Agony in the Garden—a visit which must have been the appointed means of some great strengthening of the Sacred Humanity for the terrible conflict which He was about to pass through, or, rather, which He had already in great part experienced, for the Agony was itself one of the greatest of Our Lord's sufferings. The Angel may be thought to have set before Our Lord the will of the Eternal Father as the reason for the chalice which He was to drink, the immense glory to His Father and to Himself which would accrue therefrom, the great fruit which His sufferings would produce in the souls of men, and the whole of the marvellous counsel of God in the application of the merits of His Precious Blood.

In the same way we may suppose that the Angels may comfort the Holy Souls by representing to them the decree of God's justice, which must be so dear to them, in pursuance of which they are for a time to suffer as they do—the glory which accrues to God from their undergoing the sentence of His justice, the blessed issue of their purification, which will open to them the gates of the eternal home of God's children, and the like. But it must be the most direct part of the consolation which the Holy Angels constantly minister to the souls in Purgatory to give them intelligence of the prayers and satisfactions which are offered for them in the Church on earth, and thus to let them know that they are not forgotten, and that the time of their detention is to be shortened. In this respect they are in truth messengers of good tidings and of peace, which they so much delight to be. Moreover, it is probable that the Holy Angels are the sources from whom proceed a thousand suggestions to us to pray for the Holy Souls, sudden remembrances of them, feelings as if they were near and in need of our prayers, and the like. The visions of the Saints reigning in Heaven are ordinarily the works of the Angels, and it may be that, if there be from time to time any similar visions of the souls in Purgatory, the Angels are also the artificers, so to speak, of these.

Thus we get some faint idea of the work of the Angels of the Holy Souls as of a work of active and multifarious charity, carried on with unwearied energy and vigilance, the object of the whole being to procure relief for those sufferers in all the many ways in which God allows of their being relieved. They pray for them before the throne of God, and if the Angel of Macedonia could appear to the Apostle and entreat him to come over and help him, it is not wonderful [cause for wonder] if they now implore the Saints to intercede for the Holy Souls, and also stir up the hearts of the children of the Church on earth for the same object of charity. And then at length comes the time of intense joy, both to the Angels and to the Holy Souls themselves, when the purification has been accomplished, and nothing now remains but for the souls to be presented to God by their Guardians, at the head of whom the blessed St. Michael is placed for this solemn act of triumph. It is, then, in our power to rejoice the hearts of the glorious Angels of God by the suffrages which we offer for the Holy Souls, to make them our friends, and secure their advocacy for ourselves, by making them our debtors for the charity which we have shown to those in whom they regard themselves as relieved and succored by our prayers.

Our Lord says some terrible words about those who scandalize one of the little ones who believe in Him, on account of the simple truth that their Angels always see the face of His Father. We may turn the threat which His words convey into a most gracious promise of protection and advocacy on the part of these glorious Princes of the Court of God, by praying and suffering faithfully for these Holy Souls whose Angels are always in God's presence, to bear witness to the slightest act of charity which is done for these patient sufferers.   —REV. H. J. COLERIDGE, S.J.

St. Gregory mentions with astonishment in his *Dialogues* the case of Cardinal Paschasius, who was a great friend to the poor, a generous almsgiver, a most courageous despiser of himself, and a brave champion of the Catholic Faith. He died in the odor of sanctity, and the mere touch of his coffin was enough to drive out demons, so that no one doubted that he was already in possession of heavenly glory. But how different the judgments of God from those of men! The same Paschasius a long time after, as St. Gregory says, appeared to Germanus, the holy Bishop of Capua, and mournfully begged his help, that he might at last be freed from his torments, and be admitted to the beatific vision. When asked why he was detained so long in Purgatory, he said: "For nothing else than my obstinacy in persisting in my opinion that Laurence was more worthy of the papacy than Symmachus, although Symmachus had been unanimously voted to the Apostolic See."

∾ THIRTIETH DAY ∾

A Day of Prayer for All the Faithful Departed, Especially for Those Who Died During this Month

WE have now come to the last day of the month of the Holy Souls; let us not, however, cease to interest ourselves in their behalf, but, on the contrary, let us redouble our zeal in their favor, that we may procure for ourselves the many blessings in this life and the next which are the reward of this devotion, and let us seek to engage many others in the same. It is the common opinion of the Fathers and Doctors of the Church that those who fervently and perseveringly interest themselves for the souls in Purgatory will not be lost. O security to be desired!

The extreme severity of the punishments of Purgatory is a consideration which leads the mind to contemplate the immense multitude of the saved, and of those saved with very imperfect dispositions, as the only solution of these chastisements. Purgatory goes as near to the unriddling the riddle of the world as any one ordinance of God which can be named. Difficulties are perpetually drifting that way to find their explanation; and the Saints of God have turned so full a light upon those fields of fire that the geography of them seems almost as familiar to us as the well-known features of the surface of the earth. The charitable practices of Catholic devotion lead us to spend so much of our day amid the patience of that beautiful suffering, that it has become to us like the wards of a favorite hospital, with its familiar faces brightening at the welcome words of consolation. It is the same fire as Hell. That in itself is a terrible reflection. The revelations of the Saints depict the tortures of it as fearful in the extreme. There is a consent of them as to the immense lengths of time which souls average under that punishment—a consent fully bearing out the practice of the Church in anniversaries and foundations for Masses for ever. The very slightest infidelition to grace seem to be visited there with acutest sufferings. God Himself has bidden His Saints to honor with chaste fear and exceeding awe the rigors of His justice and the requirements of His purity in that land of bitter long delay.

Now, does it come natural to us to look at all this system, this terrible "eighth sacrament" of fire, which is the home of those souls whom the seven real Sacraments of earth have not been allowed to purify completely—does it come natural to us to look at it all as simply a penal machinery invented for the Saints, and those most like the Saints, to cut away with its vindictive sharpness the little imperfections which come of human frailty? That it should fulfill this office is most intelligible, most accordant with God's perfections, and most consolatory to souls themselves. But does not the view at once recommend itself to us that it was an invention of God to multiply the fruit of our Saviour's Passion; that it

was intended for the great multitudes who should die in
charity with God, but in imperfect charity, and therefore
that it is, as it were, the continuance of deathbed mercies
beyond the grave; and that, as such, it throws no uncertain
light on the cheering supposition that most Catholics are
saved, especially of the poor, who sorrow and suffer here?

Do we ever dwell in thought on God's unaccountable contentment with so little as requisite for salvation? Of course,
Purgatory goes some way toward accounting for it, but very
far from the whole way. Purgatory seems too good for
ungenerous souls, and yet they are crowding into it by thousands, and become beautiful amid its flames. The merits
and satisfactions of our dearest Lord seem our only refuge
when we see how low it has pleased God to put the terms of
our redemption. The charity of Jesus covers the multitude
of the sins of His people. God sees the world through Him,
not simply by a fiction imputing to us the holiness that is
Our Lord's, but for His sake, and by the efficacy of His
Blood, actually ennobling our unworthiness, and giving a
real greatness to our littleness and a solid value to the mer-
est intentions of our love. It is the daily delight of His justice to be limited in the operations of its righteous anger by
the Adorable Sacrifice of the Mass; and the glory of Jesus is
the grand fundamental law of all creation.

Yet, even so, God's contentment with so little from us is
an inscrutable mercy. Who shall tell the thousands of souls
in Heaven at this hour whom, almost to their own surprise,
that marvellous contentment has exalted there? How shall
we define God's golden attribute of mercy? Is it not the one
perfection which we creatures give, or seem to give, to our
Creator? How could He have mercy, were it not for us? He
has no sorrows that want soothing, no necessities that need
supplying; for He is the ocean of interminable being. Mercy
is the tranquility of His omnipotence and the sweetness of
His omnipresence, the fruit of His eternity and the companion of His immensity, the chief satisfaction of His justice, the triumph of His wisdom and the patient
perseverance of His love. Wherever we go there is mercy—

the peaceful, active, broad, deep, endless mercy of our heavenly Father. If we work by day, we work in mercy's light; and we sleep at night in the lap of our Father's mercy. The courts of Heaven gleam with its outpoured prolific beauty. Earth is covered with it, as the waters cover the bed of the stormy sea. Purgatory is, as it were, its own separate creation, and is lighted by its silvery beams gleaming there through night and day. Even the realm of hopeless exile is less palpably dark than it would be did not some excesses of mercy's light enter even there.

How solemn and subduing is the thought of the holy kingdom of Purgatory, that realm of pain! There is no cry, no murmur; all is silent—silent as Jesus before His enemies. We shall never know how we really love Mary till we look up to her out of those deeps, those vales of dread mysterious fire. Beautiful region of the Church of God! Lovely troop of the flock of Mary! What a scene is presented to our eyes when we gaze upon that consecrated empire of sinlessness, and yet of keenest suffering! There is the beauty of those immaculate souls, and then the loveliness—yea, the worshipfulness—of their patience; the majesty of their gifts; the dignity of their solemn and chaste sufferings; the eloquence of their silence; the moonlight of Mary's throne lighting up their land of pain and unspeakable expectation; the silver-winged Angels voyaging through the deeps of that mysterious realm; and, above all, that unseen face of Jesus, which is so well remembered that it seems to be almost seen! What a sinless purity of worship is here in this liturgy of hallowed pain!

There are revelations which speak of some who are in Purgatory, but have no fire. They languish patiently detained from God, and that is enough chastisement for them. There are revelations, too, which tell of multitudes who are in no local prison, but abide their purification in the air, or by their graves, or near altars where the Blessed Sacrament is, or in the rooms of those who pray for them, or amid the scenes of their former vanity and frivolity. If silent suffering—sweetly, gracefully endured—is a thing so venerable on earth, what must this region of the Church be like? Compared with earth, its trials, doubts, exciting and depressing risks, how much more beautiful, how much more desirable, that still, calm, patient realm over which Mary is crowned as Queen and Michael is the perpetual ambassador of her mercy!   —FATHER FABER

A pious girl had long mourned the death of her unfortunate father, a zealous revolutionist, who was drowned in the River Seine in 1793 by two men, his companions in guilt; thus was he suddenly overtaken by death in the midst of a wicked life. His daughter, having retired to a village in Burgundy, there spent her days in working for the poor and in praying most perseveringly for her unfortunate father, although she had every reason to fear for his salvation. She had very little hope, but prayer was a sweet and powerful consolation to her filial, affectionate heart.

At length, after many years had elapsed, her father appeared to her one day, asking for Masses, *many* Masses to be said, for he told her he was in Purgatory, God having given him grace in his last moments to see the evil of his past life, and with a truly contrite heart to implore His mercy and forgiveness. The poor girl, comforted, went in all haste to the parish priest, and begged him to say, and to get said without delay, as many Masses as possible for her intention.

The priest hastened to comply with her request; several Masses were said daily, and some weeks later the poor man appeared again to his daughter, but this time bright and joyous. He thus addressed her: "I bless you, my child! My sufferings are at an end, and I am now going to Heaven." What consolation, what joy for the heart of this good girl! The meritorious works and prayers which she had offered, foreknown by God, had no doubt obtained for her father's guilty soul the movement of sincere contrition which had secured his eternal salvation at the hour of death.

—PÈRE FAURE, S.J., *Les Consolations du Purgatoire*

THE MONK OF MESSINA

In the year 1784 there was a terrible earthquake at Messina. Houses were thrown down, many lives were lost, the very graves were opened. The only thing which escaped was the Cathedral, and the people attributed its safety to a miracle. A few years after this event the Chevalier _____, a man of noble French family, one of whose brothers was a distinguished general officer and the other a Minister at Berlin, visited Messina for the purpose of seeing the scene of devastation, and of making researches among the monuments and ruins. He was of the Order of the Knights of Malta and a priest, a man of high character, of cultivated intellect and of great physical courage.

He arrived at Messina on a fine summer day, and getting the key of the Cathedral from the *custode*—for it was after Vespers—commenced copying the inscriptions and examining the building. His researches occupied him so long that he did not see the day was waning, and when he turned to go out by the door through which he had come he found it locked. He tried the other doors, but all were equally closed. The *custode* having let him in some hours before, and concluding he had long since gone away, had locked up the building and gone home. The priest shouted in vain; the earthquake had destroyed all the houses in the neighborhood, and there was no one to hear his cries. He had, therefore, no alternative but to submit to his fate, and make up his mind to spend the night in the Cathedral. He looked round for some place to establish himself. Everything was of marble except the Confessionals, and in one of these he ensconced himself in a tolerably comfortable chair and tried to go to sleep. Sleep, however, was not easy. The strangeness of the situation, the increasing darkness, and the superstition which the strongest mind might be supposed to feel under the circumstances, effectually banished any feeling of drowsiness.

There was a large clock in the tower of the Cathedral, the tones of which sounded more near and solemn within the building than without. The priest, with the intensity of hearing which sleeplessness gives, listened to every stroke of the clock. First ten, then the quarters; then eleven, then the quarters again; then twelve o'clock. As the last stroke of midnight died away, he perceived suddenly a light appearing at the high altar. The altar candles seemed suddenly to be lighted, and a figure in a monk's habit and cowl walked out from a niche at the back of the altar. Turning when he reached the front of the altar, the figure exclaimed in a deep and solemn voice: "Is there any priest here who will say a Mass for the repose of my soul?" No answer followed, and the monk slowly walked down the church, passing by the Confessional, where the priest saw that the face under the cowl was that of a dead man. Entire darkness followed; but when the clock struck the half-hour the same events occurred: the same light appeared, and the same figure; and the same question was asked, and no answer returned; and the same monk, illuminated by the same unearthly light, walked softly down the church.

Now the priest was a brave man, and he resolved, if the same thing occurred again, that he would answer the question and say the Mass. As the clock struck one, the altar was again lighted, the monk again appeared, and when he once more exclaimed, "Is there any Christian priest here who would say a Mass for the repose of my soul?" the priest boldly stepped out of the Confessional and replied in a firm voice, "I will." He then walked up to the altar, where he found everything prepared for the celebration, and, summoning up all his courage, celebrated the sacred rite. At its conclusion the monk spoke as follows: "For *one hundred and forty years* every night I have asked this question, and until tonight in vain. You have conferred upon me an inestimable benefit. There is nothing I would not do if I could for you in return; but there is only one thing in my power, and that is to give you notice when the hour of your own death approaches." The priest heard no more. He fell down in a swoon and was found the next morning by the *custode* very early at the foot of the altar. After a time he recovered and went away.

He returned to Venice, where he was then living, and wrote down the circumstances above related, which he also told to some of his intimate friends. He steadily asserted and maintained that he was never more wide awake or more completely in possession of his reasoning faculties than he was that night until the moment when the monk had ceased speaking. Three years afterward he called his friends together and took leave of them. They asked him if he was going on a journey. He said, "Yes; and one from which there is no return." He then told them that the night before the monk of Messina had appeared to him and told him that he was to die in three days. His friends laughed at him and told him—which was true—that he seemed perfectly well. But he persisted in his statements, made every preparation, and the third day was found dead in his bed.

This story was well known to all his friends and contemporaries. Curiously enough, on the Cathedral of Messina being restored a few years after, the skeleton of a monk was found walled up in his monk's habit and cowl, and in the very place which the priest had always described as the one from which the specter had emerged.   —LADY HERBERT

THE END

Prayers for the Souls in Purgatory

Added by TAN Books and Publishers, Inc.
Ecclesiastical Approbation, 2002.

A Prayer for the Souls in Purgatory

O MOST gentle Heart of Jesus, ever present in the Blessed Sacrament, ever consumed with burning love for the poor captive souls in Purgatory, have mercy on the souls of Thy departed servants. Be not severe in Thy judgments, but let some drops of Thy Precious Blood fall upon the devouring flames. And do Thou, O Merciful Saviour, send Thy holy angels to conduct them to a place of refreshment, light and peace. Amen.

A Prayer for the Dead

O GOD, the Creator and Redeemer of all the Faithful, grant unto the souls of Thy departed servants full remission of all their sins, that through the help of our pious supplications they may obtain that pardon which they have always desired, Thou Who lives and reigns world without end. Amen.

V. Eternal rest grant unto them, O Lord.
R. *And let perpetual light shine upon them.*
V. May they rest in peace. Amen.
R. *And may the souls of all the faithful departed, through the mercy of God, rest in peace. Amen.*

A Prayer for our Dear Departed

O GOOD Jesus, Whose loving Heart was ever troubled by the sorrows of others, look with pity on the souls of our dear ones in Purgatory. O Thou Who didst "love Thine own," hear our cry for mercy, and grant that those whom Thou hast called from our homes and hearts may soon enjoy everlasting rest in the home of Thy Love in Heaven. Amen.

V. Eternal rest grant unto them, O Lord.
R. *And let perpetual light shine upon them. Amen.*

A Prayer for Deceased Parents

O GOD, Who hast commanded us to honor our father and our mother, in Thy mercy have pity on the souls of my father and mother, and forgive them their trespasses, and make me to see them again in the joy of everlasting brightness. Through Christ our Lord. Amen.

Offering of the Precious Blood

ETERNAL Father, I offer Thee the Precious Blood of Jesus Christ in satisfaction for my sins, in supplication for the Holy Souls in Purgatory and for the needs of Holy Church. Amen.

A Prayer for the Poor Souls

MY JESUS, by the sorrows Thou didst suffer in Thine agony in the Garden, in Thy scourging and crowning with thorns, on the way to Calvary, and in Thy crucifixion and death, have mercy on the souls in Purgatory, and especially on those that are most forsaken; do Thou deliver them from the dire torments they endure; call them and admit them to Thy most sweet embrace in Paradise. Amen.

Our Father ... Hail Mary ... Glory Be ... (See p. 163.)

V. Eternal rest grant unto them, O Lord.
R. *And let perpetual light shine upon them.*
V. May the divine assistance remain always with us.
R. *And may the souls of the faithful departed, through the mercy of God, rest in peace. Amen.*

Prayer for the Poor Souls from the Canon of the Mass

REMEMBER, O Lord, Thy servants and handmaids, N. and N., who have gone before us marked with the sign of faith and rest in the sleep of peace. To these, O Lord, and to all who rest in Christ, grant, we beseech Thee, a place of comfort, light and peace. Through the same Christ our Lord. Amen.

—Roman Missal

A Prayer for a Deceased Priest

O GOD, Thou didst raise Thy servant, N., to the sacred priesthood of Jesus Christ, according to the Order of Melchisedech, giving him the sublime power to offer the Eternal Sacrifice, to bring the Body and Blood of Thy Son Jesus Christ down upon the altar, and to absolve the sins of men in Thine own holy Name. We beseech Thee to reward his faithfulness and to forget his faults, admitting him speedily into Thy holy presence, there to enjoy forever the recompense of his labors. This we ask through Jesus Christ Thy Son our Lord. Amen.

A Prayer addressed to the Poor Souls in Purgatory

O HOLY SOULS in Purgatory, thou art the certain heirs of Heaven. Thou art most dear to Jesus, as the trophies of His Precious Blood, and to Mary, Mother of Mercy. Obtain for me, through thine intercession, the grace to lead a holy life, to die a happy death, and to attain to the blessedness of eternity in Heaven.

Dear suffering souls, who long to be delivered in order to praise and glorify God in Heaven, by thine unfailing pity, help me in the needs which distress me at this time, particularly (*here mention your request*), so that I may obtain relief and assistance from God.

In gratitude for this intercession, I offer to God on thy behalf the satisfactory merits of my prayers, works, joys and sufferings of this day (*week, month, or whatever space of time you wish to designate*). Amen.

A Prayer *for* and *to* the Souls in Purgatory

O MOST compassionate Jesus, have mercy on the souls detained in Purgatory, for whose redemption Thou didst take upon Thyself our nature and endure a bitter death. Mercifully hear their sighs, look with pity upon the tears which they now shed before Thee, and by virtue of Thy Passion, release them from the pains due to their sins. O most merciful Jesus, let Thy Precious Blood reach down into Purgatory and refresh and revive the captive souls who suffer there. Stretch out to them Thy strong right hand, and bring them forth into the place of refreshment, light and peace. Amen.

O blessed souls! We have prayed for thee! We entreat thee, who art so dear to God, and who art certain of never losing Him, to pray for us poor miserable sinners who are in danger of being damned and of losing God forever. Amen.

For Our Deceased Servicemen

THOU art all-powerful, O God, and livest for-ever in light and joy. Look with pity and love, we beseech Thee, upon those men who have bravely fought and gallantly died for our country. By laying down their lives, they have showed supreme love for others. We implore Thee to accept their sacrifice and their belief in the justice of the cause for which they died. May their offering not be in vain. Deign to forgive any sins or mis-deeds they may have committed. Bring them quickly, we implore Thee, into Thine august presence, where fear, sadness, mourning and death no longer exist. Have pity, in Thy loving kindness, on those they leave behind. In Thine own inscrutable ways, make good their absence, and lavishly bestow Thy love and consolations upon those deprived of their presence. This we ask of Thee in the name of Jesus Christ, Our King. Amen.

Eternal Rest

Requiescant in pace

V. Eternal rest grant unto them, O Lord.

R. *And let perpetual light shine upon them.*

V. May they rest in peace.

R. *Amen.* *(Partial indulgence)*

Prayer of St. Gertrude the Great

O ETERNAL Father, I offer Thee the Most Pre-cious Blood of Thy Divine Son, Jesus, in union with the Masses said throughout the world today, for all the holy souls in Purgatory, and for sinners everywhere—for sinners in the Universal Church, for those in my own home and for those within my family. Amen.

A Novena for the Poor Souls

SUNDAY

O LORD God Almighty, I beseech Thee by the Precious Blood which Thy divine Son Jesus shed in the Garden, deliver the souls in Purgatory, and *especially that one which is the most forsaken of all*, and bring it into Thy glory, where it may praise and bless Thee forever. Amen.

Our Father . . . Hail Mary . . . Glory Be . . . (See p. 163.) Eternal rest grant unto them, O Lord, and let perpetual light shine upon them. May they rest in peace. Amen.

(Prayer on Every Day of the Novena, p. 162)

MONDAY

O LORD God Almighty, I beseech Thee by the Precious Blood which Thy divine Son Jesus shed in His cruel scourging, deliver the souls in Purgatory, and among them all, *especially that soul which is nearest to its entrance into Thy glory*, that it may soon begin to praise Thee and bless Thee forever. Amen.

Our Father . . . Hail Mary . . . Glory Be . . .
Eternal rest . . .
(Prayer on Every Day of the Novena, p. 162)

TUESDAY

O LORD God Almighty, I beseech Thee by the Precious Blood of Thy divine Son Jesus that was shed in His bitter crowning with thorns, deliver the souls in Purgatory, and among them all, *particularly that soul which is in the greatest need of our prayers*, in order that it may not long be delayed in praising Thee in Thy glory and blessing Thee forever. Amen.

Our Father . . . Hail Mary . . . Glory Be . . .
Eternal rest . . .
(Prayer on Every Day of the Novena, p. 162)

WEDNESDAY

O LORD God Almighty, I beseech Thee by the Precious Blood of Thy divine Son Jesus that was shed in the streets of Jerusalem, whilst He carried on His sacred shoulders the heavy burden of the Cross, deliver the souls in Purgatory, and *especially that one which is richest in merits in Thy sight,* so that, having soon attained the high place in glory to which it is destined, it may praise Thee triumphantly and bless Thee forever. Amen.

Our Father . . . Hail Mary . . . Glory Be . . .

Eternal rest . . .

(Prayer on Every Day of the Novena, p. 162)

THURSDAY

O LORD God Almighty, I beseech Thee by the Precious Blood of Thy divine Son Jesus which He Himself, on the night before His Passion, gave as meat and drink to His beloved Apostles and bequeathed to His holy Church to be the perpetual Sacrifice and life-giving nourishment of His faithful people, deliver the souls in Purgatory, *but most of all, that soul which was most devoted to this Mystery of infinite love,* in order that it may praise Thee therefore, together with Thy divine Son and the Holy Spirit in Thy glory forever. Amen.

Our Father . . . Hail Mary . . . Glory Be . . .

Eternal rest . . .

(Prayer on Every Day of the Novena, p. 162)

FRIDAY

O LORD God Almighty, I beseech Thee by the Precious Blood which Jesus Thy divine Son did shed this day upon the tree of the Cross, especially from His sacred hands and feet, deliver the souls in Purgatory, and *particularly that soul for whom I am most bound to pray,* in order that I may not be the cause which hinders Thee from admitting it quickly to the possession of Thy glory, where it may praise Thee and bless Thee for ever-more. Amen.

Our Father . . . Hail Mary . . . Glory Be . . .

Eternal rest . . .

(Prayer on Every Day of the Novena, p. 162)

(Prayer on Every Day of the Novena, p. 162)

SATURDAY

O LORD God Almighty, I beseech Thee by the Precious Blood which gushed forth from the sacred side of Thy divine Son Jesus in the presence of and to the great sorrow of His most holy Mother, deliver the souls in Purgatory, and among them all, *especially that soul which has been most devout to this noble Lady*, that it may come quickly into Thy glory, there to praise Thee in her, and her in Thee, through all the ages. Amen.

Our Father . . . Hail Mary . . . Glory Be . . .

Eternal rest . . .

(Prayer on Every Day of the Novena, p. 162)

PRAYER ON EVERY DAY OF THE NOVENA

V. O Lord, hear my prayer.

R. *And let my cry come unto Thee.*

O GOD, the Creator and Redeemer of all the faithful, grant unto the souls of Thy servants and handmaids the remission of all their sins, that through our devout supplications, they may obtain the pardon they have always desired, Who lives and reigns world without end. Amen.

Eternal rest . . .

Prayer for the Dying

O MOST Merciful Jesus, lover of souls, I pray Thee, by the agony of Thy most Sacred Heart, and by the sorrows of Thine Immaculate Mother, to wash in Thy Most Precious Blood the sinners of the whole world who are now in their agony and who will die today.

Heart of Jesus, once in agony, have mercy on the dying! Amen.

O Mother most merciful,
pray for the souls in Purgatory!

Our Father

OUR FATHER, Who art in Heaven, hallowed be Thy Name. Thy kingdom come, Thy will be done on earth as it is in Heaven. Give us this day our daily bread, and forgive us our trespasses, as we forgive those who trespass against us. And lead us not into temptation, but deliver us from evil. Amen.

Hail Mary

HAIL MARY, full of grace, the Lord is with thee; blessed art thou among women, and blessed is the fruit of thy womb, Jesus. Holy Mary, Mother of God, pray for us sinners, now and at the hour of our death. Amen.

Glory Be

GLORY BE to the Father, and to the Son, and to the Holy Ghost. As it was in the beginning, is now, and ever shall be, world without end. Amen.

How to Gain
A Plenary Indulgence

An Indulgence is the remission before God of the temporal punishment due to be suffered for sins that have already been forgiven. In granting Indulgences, the Church, as minister of the Redemption, authoritatively dispenses and applies the treasury of the satisfaction won by Christ and the Saints. The temporal punishment due for forgiven sins must be suffered either on earth or in Purgatory. A *Partial Indulgence* remits part of the temporal punishment due; a *Plenary Indulgence* remits all the temporal punishment due. Indulgences can always be offered for the Poor Souls in Purgatory, rather than for ourselves. However, Indulgences offered for the Poor Souls are efficacious by way of *suffrage*, that is, depending on God's decision, since the Church on earth does not have jurisdiction over the souls in Purgatory.

Four Ways To Gain
A Plenary Indulgence

A Catholic, being in the state of grace, can gain a *Plenary Indulgence* by many different prayers and works of piety, but these four are worthy of special mention:

1. **Making a visit to the Blessed Sacrament** to adore It for at least one half hour.

2. **Spending at least one half hour reading**

Sacred Scripture, as spiritual reading, with the veneration due to the Word of God.

3. **Making the Way of the Cross**. This includes walking from Station to Station. (At publicly held Stations, if this cannot be done in an orderly way, at least the leader must move from Station to Station.) No specific prayers are required, but devout meditation on the Passion and Death of Our Lord is required (not necessarily on the individual Stations).

4. **Recitation of the Rosary** (or at least 5 decades), with devout meditation on the Mysteries, in addition to the vocal recitation. It must be said in a church, family group, religious community or pious association.

Additional Requirements

In addition to performing the specified work, these three conditions are required:

1. Confession;
2. Holy Communion;
3. Prayer for the Holy Father's intentions. (One Our Father and one Hail Mary suffice.)

The three conditions may be fulfilled several days before or after the performance of the prescribed work; it is fitting, however, that Communion be received and the prayer for the intention of the Holy Father be recited on the same day the work is performed.

In addition, to gain a Plenary Indulgence, a person's mind and heart must be free from all attachment to sin, even venial sin.

If one tries to gain a Plenary Indulgence, but fails to fulfill all the requirements, the indulgence will be only partial.

Only one Plenary Indulgence may be gained per day, except that, at "the moment of death," a person may gain a second Plenary Indulgence for *that* day.

If we generously offer Indulgences for the Holy Souls in Purgatory, we may hope to obtain relief or release for many of them, in accord with God's holy Will. In gratitude, they may well obtain for us many great favors.

The norms given here are from the official *Enchiridion of Indulgences* (1968) and the Apostolic Constitution *The Doctrine of Indulgences* (1967).

APPROBATION FOR "HOW TO GAIN A PLENARY INDULGENCE"

Nihil Obstat:
   Reverend Monsignor Charles W. McNamee, S.T.L., J.C.L.
   Censor Librorum

Imprimatur:
   ✠Most Reverend Thomas G. Doran, D.D., J.C.D.
   Bishop of Rockford
   March 31, 1998

The *Nihil Obstat* and *Imprimatur* are official declarations that a book or pamphlet is free from doctrinal or moral error. No implications are contained therein that those who have granted the *Nihil Obstat* or *Imprimatur* agree with the contents, opinions or statements expressed.

The *Dies Irae*

From the traditional Requiem Mass. The Dies Irae *is an impassioned outpouring of the Catholic heart. It expresses fear and hope.*

Day of wrath and doom impending,
David's word with Sibyl's blending,
Heaven and earth in ashes ending.

O what fear man's bosom rendeth,
When from heaven the Judge descendeth,
On whose sentence all dependeth.

Wondrous sound the trumpet flingeth,
Through earth's sepulchres it ringeth,
All before the throne it bringeth.

Death is struck, and nature quaking,
All creation is awaking,
To its Judge an answer making.

Lo, the book exactly worded,
Wherein all hath been recorded,
Thence shall judgement be awarded.

When the Judge His seat attaineth,
And each hidden deed arraigneth,
Nothing unavenged remaineth.

What shall I, frail man, be pleading?
Who for me be interceding
When the just are mercy needing?

King of majesty tremendous,
Who dost free salvation send us,
Fount of pity, then befriend us.

Think, kind Jesus, my salvation
Caused Thy wondrous Incarnation,
Leave me not to reprobation.

Faint and weary Thou hast sought me,
On the Cross of suffering bought me,
Shall such grace be vainly brought me?

Righteous Judge, for sin's pollution
Grant Thy gift of absolution,
Ere that day of retribution.

Guilty now I pour my moaning,
All my shame with anguish owning.
Spare, O God, Thy suppliant groaning.

Through the sinful Mary shriven,
Through the dying thief forgiven,
Thou to me a hope hast given.

Worthless are my prayers and sighing,
Yet, good Lord, in grace complying,
Rescue me from fires undying.

With Thy sheep a place provide me,
From the goats afar divide me,
To Thy right hand do Thou guide me.

When the wicked are confounded,
Doomed to flames of woe unbounded,
Call me with Thy Saints surrounded.

Low I kneel with heart's submission,
See, like ashes, my contrition,
Help me in my last condition.

Ah! that day of tears and mourning,
From the dust of earth returning,
Man for judgment must prepare him,
Spare, O God, in mercy spare him.

Lord, all-pitying, Jesus blest,
Grant them Thine eternal rest.

Amen.

Thorough, traditional, up-to-date, easy to read and highly informative!! . . .

THIS IS THE FAITH
A Complete Explanation of the Catholic Faith
By Fr. Francis J. Ripley

- Very practical to use and easy to read.
- Satisfies people at all levels of knowledge about Catholicism.
- Contains the classic Catholic doctrinal and moral teachings.
- Highly interesting, page after page!
- No trendy or wishy-washy writing.
- Originally published in 1951.
- Newly brought up to date with current Church disciplines in 2002.
- 100,000 sold in 11 months!!
- The complete original book is still virtually intact in this edition, but with slight corrections—plus, many amplifications and some additional material.
- **This has to be the best, most reliable, most readable Catholic adult catechism in print today!!!**
- Was also a great college freshman religion text.
- Perfect for inquirers, converts, fallen-away Catholics, those weak in their Faith and even practicing Catholics who want a thorough review!

No. 1578. 474 Pp.
PB. Impr.
ISBN 0-89555-642-1

21.00

2 copies $30.00
3 copies $39.00
5 copies $50.00
(5 or more copies—
$10.00 each)

No. 2000   MP3-CD
Audiobook
21 Hrs. Same prices as above. Combine books and MP3-CD's.

Prices subject to change.

TAN BOOKS AND PUBLISHERS, INC.
P.O. Box 424 • Rockford, Illinois 61105

Toll Free 1-800-437-5876
Tel 815-226-7777

Fax 815-226-7770
www.tanbooks.com

Finally, a wonderful, practical Catholic Bible Commentary for everyone!!

A PRACTICAL COMMENTARY ON HOLY SCRIPTURE

By Bishop Frederick Justus Knecht, D.D.

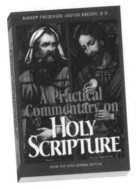

No. 1882. 284 Pp. PB.
Imprimatur 1923.
ISBN 0-89555-757-6.
Reg. 40.00

Now Only 30.00

Prices subject to change.

This book is a great introductory Bible study all by itself—for it brings out the Catholic teachings that are hidden in Sacred Scripture! A famous book which went through at least 16 editions and was recommended by 14 bishops, this commentary is not a work for scholars, but rather *a very practical book for the "ordinary"* Catholic. It hands on to new generations the classic meaning of famous, important Scriptural passages—from both Old Testament and New Testament—in a manner that is easy to understand.

A typical chapter will first tell the Bible story, based on the Douay-Rheims Bible, with many fascinating explanations of particular words and phrases. Then follow many brief explanations of topics in the Scripture passage, showing clearly the Catholic doctrines that are contained there. Finally, a brief "Application" to daily life is given in each chapter. (Some of these are aimed at youth, yet overall they apply to everyone.) *A Practical Commentary* will soon convince the reader that the Bible is a Catholic book.

Every Catholic, every Catholic classroom, home school, catechist and priest should have a well-used copy of *A Practical Commentary on Holy Scripture*!

Easy to understand. Highly Informative. Totally Catholic!!

TAN BOOKS AND PUBLISHERS, INC.
P.O. Box 424 • Rockford, Illinois 61105

Toll Free 1-800-437-5876
Tel 815-226-7777

Fax 815-226-7770
www.tanbooks.com

A powerful confirmation of faith . . .

EUCHARISTIC MIRACLES

AND EUCHARISTIC PHENOMENA
IN THE LIVES OF THE SAINTS

By Joan Carroll Cruz

No. 1047. 305 Pp.
PB. Impr. 123 Illus.
ISBN 0-89555-303-1

16.50

Prices subject to change.

Describes over 40 of the Church's most astounding Eucharistic miracles: Hosts which have bled, levitated, become hard as flint when received by a person in mortal sin, etc. Plus, saints who experienced levitations, visions, phenomena of tears, fire or light when receiving Communion, saints who lived on the Eucharist as their only food, saints who received Holy Communion miraculously, and other Eucharistic miracles in the lives of the Saints. Features 123 illustrations, including photos. Powerful confirmation of the truth of the Catholic Faith!

TAN BOOKS AND PUBLISHERS, INC.
P.O. Box 424 • Rockford, Illinois 61105

Toll Free 1-800-437-5876
Tel 815-226-7777

Fax 815-226-7770
www.tanbooks.com

One of the most fascinating books ever . . .

THE INCORRUPTIBLES

A Study of the Incorruption of the Bodies of Various Catholic Saints and Beati

By Joan Carroll Cruz

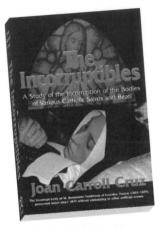

**No. 0199. 310 Pp.
PB. Impr. 33 Illus.
ISBN 0-89555-066-0**

16.50

Prices subject to change.

The stories of 102 canonized Saints and Beati whose bodies were found incorrupt long after their deaths, many of which remained fresh and flexible for years, or even centuries. Many endured abnormally adverse conditions in remaining intact, e.g., damp graves—or such as St. Francis Xavier's, which was buried in lime for quick decomposition. Also goes into heavenly fragrances, the exuding of holy oil and the flow of fresh blood several years after death. Includes St. Cecilia, St. Rita, the Curé of Ars, St. Bernadette, and many more. A fascinating, documented study which will reinforce one's faith in the Catholic Church—the only religion that possesses the phenomenon of bodily incorruption. Belongs in every Catholic home.

TAN BOOKS AND PUBLISHERS, INC.
P.O. Box 424 • Rockford, Illinois 61105

**Toll Free 1-800-437-5876
Tel 815-226-7777**

**Fax 815-226-7770
www.tanbooks.com**

Surprisingly popular . . .

HELL
PLUS HOW TO AVOID HELL
By Fr. F. X. Schouppe, S.J. *and* Thomas A. Nelson

No. 0225. 488 Pp. PB.
ISBN 0-89555-346-5

15.00
Prices subject to change.

Frightening stories from history, exemplifying the existence of Hell, plus the essential steps to avoid going there. Excellent to give non-Catholics and fallen-away Catholics, but also great for practicing Catholics. Carries a knock-out punch. This book has helped many people to know their Faith as never before and to return to practicing it. One priest called this the best, most complete popular catechism he had seen! A book to help people find eternal salvation. (5—$8.00 ea.; 10—$7.00 ea.)

CONFESSION—Its Fruitful Practice
With an Examination of Conscience

Explains in remarkable detail all about Confession, including the Five Things Necessary for a Good Confession, false consciences and their remedies, Perfect and Imperfect Contrition, occasions of sin, sacrilegious Confession, General Confession, prayers before and after, etc. Includes An Easy Method of Going to Confession and a wonderful Examination of Conscience. A most valuable booklet, packed with traditional Catholic teachings! (5—$1.50 ea.; 10—$1.25 ea.; 25—$1.00 ea.; 50—$.80 ea.; 100—$.70 ea.; 500—$.60 ea.; 1,000—$.50 ea.)

No. 1723. 74 Pp.
PB. Imprimatur.
ISBN 0-89555-675-8

3.00
Prices subject to change.

TAN BOOKS AND PUBLISHERS, INC.
P.O. Box 424 • Rockford, Illinois 61105

Toll Free 1-800-437-5876
Tel 815-226-7777

Fax 815-226-7770
www.tanbooks.com

If you have enjoyed this book, consider making your next selection from among the following . . .

Prices subject to change.

Prices subject to change.

Seven Capital Sins. *Benedictine Sisters* 3.00
Confession—Its Fruitful Practice. *Ben. Srs.* 3.00
Sermons of the Curé of Ars. *Vianney* 15.00
St. Antony of the Desert. *St. Athanasius* 7.00
Is It a Saint's Name? *Fr. William Dunne* 3.00
St. Pius V—His Life, Times, Miracles. *Anderson* 7.00
Who Is Therese Neumann? *Fr. Charles Carty.* 3.50
Martyrs of the Coliseum. *Fr. O'Reilly.* 21.00
Way of the Cross. *St. Alphonsus Liguori* 1.50
Way of the Cross. *Franciscan version* 1.50
How Christ Said the First Mass. *Fr. Meagher* 21.00
Too Busy for God? Think Again! *D'Angelo* 7.00
St. Bernadette Soubirous. *Trochu* 21.00
Pope Pius VII. *Anderson* 16.50
Treatise on the Love of God. 1 Vol. *de Sales. Mackey, Trans.* 27.50
Confession Quizzes. *Radio Replies Press* 2.50
St. Philip Neri. *Fr. V. J. Matthews.* 7.50
St. Louise de Marillac. *Sr. Vincent Regnault* 7.50
The Old World and America. *Rev. Philip Furlong* 21.00
Prophecy for Today. *Edward Connor* 7.50
The Book of Infinite Love. *Mother de la Touche* 7.50
Chats with Converts. *Fr. M. D. Forrest.* 13.50
The Church Teaches. *Church Documents* 18.00
Conversation with Christ. *Peter T. Rohrbach* 12.50
Purgatory and Heaven. *J. P. Arendzen.* 6.00
Liberalism Is a Sin. *Sarda y Salvany* 9.00
Spiritual Legacy of Sr. Mary of the Trinity. *van den Broek* 13.00
The Creator and the Creature. *Fr. Frederick Faber* 17.50
Radio Replies. 3 Vols. *Frs. Rumble and Carty* 48.00
Convert's Catechism of Catholic Doctrine. *Fr. Geiermann* 5.00
Incarnation, Birth, Infancy of Jesus Christ. *St. Alphonsus* 13.50
Light and Peace. *Fr. R. P. Quadrupani* 8.00
Dogmatic Canons & Decrees of Trent, Vat. I. *Documents.* 11.00
The Evolution Hoax Exposed. *A. N. Field* 9.00
The Primitive Church. *Fr. D. I. Lanslots.* 12.50
The Priest, the Man of God. *St. Joseph Cafasso* 16.00
Blessed Sacrament. *Fr. Frederick Faber* 20.00
Christ Denied. *Fr. Paul Wickens* 3.50
New Regulations on Indulgences. *Fr. Winfrid Herbst* 3.00
A Tour of the Summa. *Msgr. Paul Glenn* 22.50
Latin Grammar. *Scanlon and Scanlon* 18.00
A Brief Life of Christ. *Fr. Rumble* 3.50
Marriage Quizzes. *Radio Replies Press* 2.50
True Church Quizzes. *Radio Replies Press.* 2.50
The Secret of the Rosary. *St. Louis De Montfort.* 5.00
Mary, Mother of the Church. *Church Documents* 5.00
The Sacred Heart and the Priesthood. *de la Touche* 10.00
Revelations of St. Bridget. *St. Bridget of Sweden* 4.50
Magnificent Prayers. *St. Bridget of Sweden* 2.00
The Happiness of Heaven. *Fr. J. Boudreau.* 10.00
St. Catherine Labouré of the Miraculous Medal. *Dirvin* 16.50
The Glories of Mary. *St. Alphonsus Liguori* 21.00
Three Conversions/Spiritual Life. *Garrigou-Lagrange, O.P.* 7.00

Prices subject to change.

St. Margaret Clitherow—"The Pearl of York." *Monro*.................... 6.00
St. Vincent Ferrer. *Fr. Pradel, O.P.*................................ 9.00
The Life of Father De Smet. *Fr. Laveille, S.J.* 18.00
Glories of Divine Grace. *Fr. Matthias Scheeben*.....................18.00
Holy Eucharist—Our All. *Fr. Lukas Etlin*........................... 3.00
Hail Holy Queen (from *Glories of Mary*). *St. Alphonsus* 9.00
Novena of Holy Communions. *Lovasik* 2.50
Brief Catechism for Adults. *Cogan*..................................12.50
The Cath. Religion—Illus./Expl. for Child, Adult, Convert. *Burbach* 12.50
Eucharistic Miracles. *Joan Carroll Cruz*...........................16.50
The Incorruptibles. *Joan Carroll Cruz* 16.50
Secular Saints: 250 Lay Men, Women & Children. PB. *Cruz*............35.00
Pope St. Pius X. *F. A. Forbes* 11.00
St. Alphonsus Liguori. *Frs. Miller and Aubin*.......................18.00
Self-Abandonment to Divine Providence. *Fr. de Caussade, S.J.* 22.50
The Song of Songs—A Mystical Exposition. *Fr. Arintero, O.P.* 21.50
Prophecy for Today. *Edward Connor* 7.50
Saint Michael and the Angels. *Approved Sources* 9.00
Dolorous Passion of Our Lord. *Anne C. Emmerich*....................18.00
Modern Saints—Their Lives & Faces, Book I. *Ann Ball*................21.00
Modern Saints—Their Lives & Faces, Book II. *Ann Ball*...............23.00
Our Lady of Fatima's Peace Plan from Heaven. *Booklet*................ 1.00
Divine Favors Granted to St. Joseph. *Père Binet*..................... 7.50
St. Joseph Cafasso—Priest of the Gallows. *St. John Bosco*............. 6.00
Catechism of the Council of Trent. *McHugh/Callan*...................27.50
The Foot of the Cross. *Fr. Faber*...................................18.00
The Rosary in Action. *John Johnson* 12.00
Padre Pio—The Stigmatist. *Fr. Charles Carty* 16.50
Why Squander Illness? *Frs. Rumble & Carty*......................... 4.00
Fatima—The Great Sign. *Francis Johnston* 12.00
Heliotropium—Conformity of Human Will to Divine *Drexelius* 15.00
Charity for the Suffering Souls. *Fr. John Nageleisen* 18.00
Devotion to the Sacred Heart of Jesus. *Verheylezoon* 16.50
Who Is Padre Pio? *Radio Replies Press* 3.00
The Stigmata and Modern Science. *Fr. Charles Carty* 2.50
St. Anthony—The Wonder Worker of Padua. *Stoddard*................. 7.00
The Precious Blood. *Fr. Faber* 16.50
The Holy Shroud & Four Visions. *Fr. O'Connell* 3.50
Clean Love in Courtship. *Fr. Lawrence Lovasik* 4.50
The Secret of the Rosary. *St. Louis De Montfort*..................... 5.00
The History of Antichrist. *Rev. P. Huchede*......................... 4.00
Where We Got the Bible. *Fr. Henry Graham* 8.00
Hidden Treasure—Holy Mass. *St. Leonard*.......................... 7.50
Imitation of the Sacred Heart of Jesus. *Fr. Arnoudt* 18.50
The Life & Glories of St. Joseph. *Edward Thompson*.................16.50
Père Lamy. *Biver*..15.00
Humility of Heart. *Fr. Cajetan da Bergamo* 9.00
The Curé D'Ars. *Abbé Francis Trochu*..............................24.00
Love, Peace and Joy. (St. Gertrude). *Prévot* 8.00

At your Bookdealer or direct from the Publisher.
Toll-Free 1-800-437-5876   **Fax 815-226-7770**
Tel. 815-229-7777   *www.tanbooks.com*

Prices subject to change.